ます # Reckless GRACE

The gift. The mystery. The embrace.

BILL VANDERBUSH
AND
BRIT EATON

Reckless Grace: The gift. The mystery. The embrace.
Copyright © 2018 by Bill Vanderbush and Brit Eaton.

All rights reserved. No part of this publication may be reproduced, distributed or transmitted in any form or by any means, including photocopying, recording, or other electronic or mechanical methods, without the prior written permission of the publisher, except in the case of brief quotations embodied in critical reviews and certain other noncommercial uses permitted by copyright law. For permission requests, write to the authors via the contact pages on the websites below.

www.billvanderbush.com
www.briteaton.com

Unless otherwise indicated, all Scripture quotations are taken from the New American Standard Bible® (NASB), Copyright © 1960, 1962, 1963, 1968, 1971, 1972, 1973, 1975, 1977, 1995 by The Lockman Foundation. Used by permission. www.Lockman.org.

Scripture quotations marked (NIV) are taken from the Holy Bible, New International Version®, NIV®. Copyright © 1973, 1978, 1984, 2011 by Biblica, Inc.™ Used by permission of Zondervan. All rights reserved worldwide. www.zondervan.com The "NIV" and "New International Version" are trademarks registered in the United States Patent and Trademark Office by Biblica, Inc.™

Scripture quotations marked NKJV are taken from the New King James Version®. Copyright © 1982 by Thomas Nelson. Used by permission. All rights reserved.

Scripture quotations marked KJV are taken from the King James Version Bible, which is in the public domain.

Scripture quotations marked CPG are taken from the Cotton Patch Gospel. Copyright © 2004 by Smyth & Helwys. Used by permission. All rights reserved.

Scripture quotations marked TMB are taken from The Mirror Bible – THE MIRROR: The Bible translated from the original text and paraphrased in contemporary speech with commentary. Copyright © 2014 by Francois du Toit. All rights reserved. Scripture taken from THE MIRROR. Copyright © 2014. Used by permission of The Author.

Scripture quotations marked INT are taken from The Interlinear Hebrew Greek English Bible. Copyright © Interlinear Bible © 2011 - 2013 by Biblos.com in cooperation with Helps Ministries. Section Headings Courtesy INT Bible © 2012, Used by Permission.

Scripture quotations marked "MSG" are taken from The Message, Copyright © 1993, 1994, 1995, 1996, 2000, 2001, 2002 by Eugene H. Peterson. Used by permission of NavPress. All rights reserved. Represented by Tyndale House Publishers, Inc.

Editing, typesetting: Sally Hanan of Inksnatcher.com
Cover photo: https://www.123rf.com/profile_nejron
Brit's head shot: Kate Caston
Bill's head shot: Ben Passmore

Ordering Information:
Quantity sales. Special discounts are available on quantity purchases by corporations, associations, and others. For details, contact Bill Vanderbush via his website, www.billvanderbush.

Reckless Grace: The gift. The mystery. The embrace/Bill Vanderbush and Brit Eaton
ISBN 9781730984952

To Traci. My soul is healed by being with you.

To Britain and Sara. It is impossible to imagine my life without both of you. There is a love that only appears as those who call you "Dad" grow older. Language is incapable of describing my love for you that warms me to life in every moment of my day. Watching you both journey into your destiny has been my greatest joy. I bless your quest into the Father's heart.

To Jesus. It is the greatest desire of my existence that You would manifest Yourself strong to my children all the days of their lives. May they know You more intimately than I have imagined and prayed.

Contents

PART I THE GRACE MESSAGE
1. Grace Redefined 3
2. Grace Received 21
3. Grace Released 35
4. Grace of God 49

PART II THE COST OF GRACE
5. The Problem with Grace 65
6. Count the Cost of Grace 87
7. Pillars of Grace 105

PART III GRACE AND GLORY
8. Grace in Action 121
9. Opportunities for Grace 131
10. The Embrace of Grace 137

About Bill 159
About Brit 161

FOREWORD

Fallen from grace. Every time a prominent figure is involved in a scandal, this phrase gets tossed around like a declaration that balance has been restored to the universe and someone who rose beyond his or her proper place got humbled. If you've ever needed grace just to feel like you're worthy to breathe again, this book will be life to you. If you've thought grace was merely God's medicine for the morally sick, then put this book away until you find yourself broken on the wheels of living. You see, grace is not something you fall from but Someone you fall into.

When I meditated deeply on this reality many years ago, feeling the overwhelming peace of God flood my heart, I revisited the Gospel of John and saw with fresh eyes verses I had ignored. It was that part of the gospel that suggested that I was included in Christ, intrinsically entwined with His death, burial, and resurrection. John 14:20 overwhelmed me with promise. "In that day you will know that I am in My Father, and you in Me, and I in you." By the time I got to John 20:23, I knew I was in unfamiliar territory. Exploring the forgotten parts of the Bible, those sections between the ones you've highlighted, can be a priceless and glorious moment of revelation. John 20:23 and John 14:20 have since been my life message.

I don't believe I've preached a sermon in the last ten years where one or both of those verses were not included in some way. The message has set captives and prisoners free, unmasked hidden lifestyles, released tears that haven't flowed in decades, unlocked healing and wholeness where hope was gone, and opened the door of salvation to thousands to hear the words, *Welcome home.* The challenge before me that was repeated often by people was that I needed to put this in a book.

"Give it away, Bill." I couldn't shake that phrase. Every time I sat down to write this book, no matter what I tried it was futile. First I tried to type it, but my fingers would freeze on the keyboard. *Perhaps writing it longhand would work*, but the pen would tremble in my hand. *Maybe if I dictated it*, but the words wouldn't come. How do you have something placed into your hands and heart and then, when it comes time to commit it to print, you can't find the grace to write a book on . . . grace?

In 2015 I was given the beautiful honor of writing a book with a dear friend and brother Ted Dekker. The message of identity and union was one we shared, and in collaborating, he was gracious enough to invite someone virtually unknown by comparison to share a writing credit. Now I found myself in a position to pay it forward by inviting someone to share in giving this message away, but where would I find that person? My wife, Traci, is an outstanding writer and had more exposure to this message than anyone else, so she seemed like the obvious option. But her work on her own novels and children's books was an overwhelming focus for her, and I knew that this had to get out of my own house.

Traveling with my friend Dale across Ohio, on the way to speak at a church, he expressed what so many had repeated: this message needed to be a book. As I explained my difficulty in trying to do just that, he went on to say, "You need a professional ghostwriter." We arrived at the church, and that day I was introduced to Brit Eaton, who turned out to be a professional ghostwriter. I was intrigued, since that's not an occupation one runs into often. She knew the message, carried the joy, and had the skill to put this out there in the way I had always envisioned. But the most important thing here was that she could take this message, and, rather than transcribe it word for word, could make this her own. As a result, this book is Brit Eaton's language and interpretation of my life's message of grace, identity, and union. It's my greatest joy to launch and empower others to run where I may have no opportunity to go. In reading through the manuscript, I was delighted to see how Brit received, interpreted, and applied the message to her life and language. And now she has imparted it back to me and all of you with her unique brand of conversational wit and spiritual wisdom. I believe she has proven what I had always hoped: that the message of the grace of God can be made personal to everyone who surrenders to fall into Him.

Bill

Confession: The first time I heard Bill Vanderbush preach on grace, I was *offended*. As Bill spoke to a crowd of thousands in Harrisburg, Pennsylvania, I knew his words were for me. But I didn't dare receive them. Even if I wanted to, how could I *possibly* forgive the mounting offenses against me when I wasn't convinced *I* was forgiven? It seemed risky, irresponsible — *reckless even*. I didn't yet understand the grace and peace he carried, but I knew I wanted it.

In months and years that followed, Holy Spirit-led grace overwhelmed me. God released me from decades of bondage and faithfully restored every broken part of my life — my marriage and family, my mental and physical health, and my true identity as a daughter of the King of heaven and a coheir with Jesus Christ. Out of that new identity, God ushered me into a season of breakthrough. He birthed new ministries, cultivated new discipling opportunities, and launched a new writing business that transformed my career into a calling.

On the heels of a whirlwind trip to Israel and Palestine for missions, a fellow traveler shared an opportunity to hear Bill speak near my home in central Ohio. I admitted to my friend Kelli on the drive over that I wondered if there might be an opportunity to do some writing work with Bill's ministry. "I've followed his teaching for years; *why else* would he be here?" I joked. Kelli told me exactly what I would have told her, "Just go up and talk to him!" Feeling insecure, I told her if this was of God, *he* would have to approach *me*. I wasn't about to insert myself without a clear leading. Thankfully, God has quite the sense of humor and didn't seem to mind my little test.

To my amazement, after the message, Bill and his friend Dale bypassed the receiving line and walked straight over to introduce themselves. We talked excitedly about what God was doing in our lives, and Dale mentioned a recent conversation about a book Bill needed to write. My jaw dropped, and Kelli giggled, "*Oh*, did you know Brit's a ghostwriter?"

In the following weeks, *Reckless Grace* emerged as the message God wanted to reveal in our unquestionably offense-obsessed culture. Needless to say, I was all in this time around. I was humbled beyond words when Bill asked me to step out of my ghostwriter role to coauthor this work with him publicly, pairing the fruits of my own grace encounter with his transformative life message. Bill truly is a hero maker and a grace conduit in the kingdom, and I'm so honored to have him as my big brother in Christ.

In the pages that follow, you'll encounter a fresh revelation of the love of God and the unthinkable grace that comes along with it. You'll revel in Bill's comprehensive case for grace — his spoken words and unmistakable voice via my written words. You'll walk through practical applications of grace that will undoubtedly change your life and relationships. Finally, you'll catch a glimpse of the grace-filled future you're being invited into — a *grace revolution* in the body of Christ.

And once you discover the *fullness* of God's reckless grace? You're going to want to spend the rest of your life giving it away.

Brit

Introduction

The scandal of grace is offensive, for it reveals the uncomfortable reality that the redemptive power of God is able to take everyone from wicked Old Testament kings like Manasseh to religious New Testament Pharisees like Paul and restore them. To the self-righteous, the gospel is offensive. To the rest of us, it's resurrection power.

To launch you into the revelation of new covenant grace, I want to take you to the old covenant prayer God gave to the priests (Numbers 6). God told the priests to ask Him to bless the people with a declaration that includes the phrase "be gracious."

> The Lord spoke to Moses, saying, "Speak to Aaron and to his sons, saying, 'Thus you shall bless the sons of Israel. You shall say to them:
>
> The Lord bless you, and keep you;
>
> The Lord make His face shine on you,
>
> And be gracious to you;
>
> The Lord lift up His countenance on you,
>
> And give you peace.'
>
> So they shall invoke My name on the sons of Israel, and I then will bless them."
>
> — Numbers 6:22–27

It's an odd thing to consider that God would wait for us to care enough about another to ask Him to do what we know is in His heart to do. Why make us the broker? He's good, and we have a hard time caring about those who need grace, so keep us out of it! But even in the New Testament, Jesus issues the challenge once again to take ownership of releasing grace to others (John 20:23). The challenge is daunting. Can you care enough about another person to ask God to bless, keep, smile upon, and give grace to another person? Every time someone asked God for grace or mercy, it was released in some measure. Perhaps one of the reasons we don't see a lot of grace in the old covenant is that the priests neglected to release the declaration they were told to release. Freely we release what we have freely been given.

Our inability to release grace demonstrates that we don't fully know *how much* we've been given. Our criticism of grace as a weak message or a license to sin demonstrates that we don't even know *what* we've been freely given. If you want the praise and applause of man, preach judgment. But if you want to get criticized, preach grace, undiluted, in all its power and love.

When all is said and done, there are really only three questions worth considering for every human being.

1. Have you been born again?
2. Have you been filled with the Holy Spirit?
3. Are you being filled right now?

Without the grace of Christ, without the reality of your reconciled union in Him, these questions would be impossible to answer. You can't work your way into them. You can't strive to be worthy to say yes to any of them. It's only by the grace of God that any of us have the ability to say yes to any of these, and it's through the grace of God that we surrender to being overtaken by this love. It's my prayer that in this book you will be taken on a journey of answering these questions with a resounding *yes*.

Bill Vanderbush

PART I

THE GRACE MESSAGE

Grace is, in my opinion, the most powerful evangelistic tool the church of Jesus Christ has never used. Individually and corporately, we cling to our offenses in a fit of so-called "righteous anger," and we completely miss out on an opportunity to witness God's grace in action. It needs to change. Now.

It's from a place of both great humility and strong authority that I share these truths with you as one who has both received and released the grace of God. The joy that comes with being a steward of God's relentless, radical, reckless grace is simply too good not to share, and so important, I'm willing to risk it all to do so.

Building a case for grace in an offense-filled world isn't for the faint of heart. And yet, by the grace of God, here I go. Here we go, together.

1 Grace Redefined

*If you forgive the sins of any, their
sins have been forgiven them; if you retain
the sins of any, they have been retained.*
— John 20:23

GRACE REDEFINED

MOST DEPRESSING PRAYER MEETING *EVER*

It's been three unbearable days. The disciples are huddled together in a secret room having the most depressing prayer meeting in history. Why? Jesus — their rabbi, master, and friend — just *died*.

His death shouldn't have come as a shock to them. Jesus *often* predicted His own death and resurrection (throughout the Gospels). But nobody *really* expected it to happen. Scripture tells us the disciples never fully grasped the literality of Jesus's words, and they were afraid to ask Him about it (Luke 9:45).

And now, the raw reality of Jesus's *quite literal* death is more than they can take. With the law on their backs and their Messiah slain, they have nothing left but one another. So they hide, without a hope left in the world.

And suddenly, the *unthinkable* happens. Out of nowhere, they hear a familiar voice . . .

"Peace to you."

Jesus *appears* to them in the flesh and says, "Peace to you," which is what you would *have* to say if you appeared in the middle of a locked room to a group of people who thought you were dead! He has to say it *twice*, which gives us a clue to the physical and emotional responses He must have triggered. Fear. Shock. Disbelief. And then? Wild amazement. Unspeakable joy. Laughter, tears, and warm embraces. As plot twists go, this was one for the history books. Christ is risen, just as He said!

It is finished — sin and death are *done*. But Jesus is just getting started.

GRACE REDEFINED

A DIVINE CONVERGENCE OF HEAVEN AND EARTH

When the disciples' initial shock begins to wear off, Jesus does something really strange. He *breathes* on them.

Christians have prayed prayers and sung songs about this in worship for centuries. You may have cut your proverbial teeth on timeless hymns like this one (Hatch, Edwin, "Breathe on Me, Breath of God.").

Breathe on me breath of God,

fill me with life anew,

that I may love as you would love,

and do what you would do.

Or perhaps you caught a vibe in contemporary worship ballads like the one by Jesus Culture that asks God to blow His mighty breath and move throughout the room in power and grace (McClarney, Chris. "Blow Mighty Breath of God.")

We sing along with these lyrics. We raise our hands, tears flow, and our hearts are moved to the rhythm of the Holy Spirit. But the breath concept remains abstract. How *unusual* would it be to have Jesus stand before you, risen and whole, and *breathe on you?* Here's how unusual: Only *twice* in Scripture does God breathe on anybody. After the dawn of creation and after the dawn of the resurrection of Jesus Christ.

Take a stroll with me back in the garden of Eden. It's the sixth day of creation – when God makes man. "Then the Lord God formed man of dust from the ground, and breathed into his nostrils the breath of life; and man became a living being" (Genesis 2:7). God forms man by speaking to the very environment of Himself when He says,

Grace Redefined

"Let Us make man in Our image, according to Our likeness" (Genesis 1:26). He uses His breath to infuse His own image and likeness into our physical being. He bends down to the earth in a symbolic (yet *very* literal) gesture; scoops together mud, dirt, and dust; and releases the life-giving breath of His spirit into it. And from this holy breath comes the first "Adam," given from the Hebrew word '*adamah* (אֲדָמָה) whose name means simply "earth." Gotta love that *sparkling* Hebrew wordplay.

God never breathes into the nostril of an animal, a plant, or any other created thing. By God's own breath, we were set apart at creation. He saved His best for last in us. And now we are animated by His breath, life, and spirit, walking in the DNA of our Creator.

Let me be clear. This is *not* a deification of man. You are not God. Got that? Good. But you *are* a beautifully created being, and *in you* rests *a divine convergence* of heaven and earth, which cements your identity as a child of God.

Grace Released in an Upper Room

Let's make our way east of Eden to another garden – Gethsemane. Before He goes to the cross, Jesus prays a prayer setting the stage for another God-breathed, divine convergence moment in the upper room. He prays for His disciples, but He doesn't stop there.

> As You sent Me into the world, I also have sent them into the world. For their sakes I sanctify Myself, that they themselves also may be sanctified in truth.
>
> I do not ask on behalf of these alone, but for those also who believe in Me through their word; that they may all be one; even as You, Father, *are* in

GRACE REDEFINED

Me and I in You, that they also may be in Us, so that the world may believe that You sent Me.
— John 17:18–21

Did you catch that? He prays for *you*. Before you were even born, Jesus, the Savior of the world, prayed for you, for me, and for all who would believe in Him through the word of the disciples. Why? That we would all be one. In His last moments, Jesus pleads to the Father for the sake of our unity — unity that can only be found through His gift of forgiveness and grace.

Flash forward once again to the upper room, mere *days* after He prays this prayer. Jesus stands before His disciples, representing *you*, *me*, and all believers. He breathes on them and says, "Receive the Holy Spirit."

When He breathes on man this second time, Jesus — the last Adam — is restoring God's image and likeness back into His creation.

But what Jesus says next is downright *shocking*. It's a life verse for me and the reason you're reading this book. After more than a decade of preaching on this verse, it still offends my mind. But this passage is the scriptural linchpin for God's grace gift, and I have no other option but to share it with you. I pray it stirs your heart and changes not only *your* life, but the lives of those around you who desperately need God's grace.

"If you forgive the sins of any, their sins have been forgiven them; if you retain the sins of any, they have been retained."
— John 20:23

Grace Redefined

Wait. *Wait.* We were doing just fine until now. What did Jesus just say? Pause for a moment and read it again. Let His words soak in. If you *forgive* others' sins . . . they're *forgiven.* If you *don't forgive* them, they're *not forgiven.*

I can imagine what you might be thinking right now. The disciples may have been thinking it back then too. *Hold up,* Jesus. *Only God* has the power to forgive sins. But *where* did you hear that? *Who told you* only God has the power to forgive sins? Maybe we choose to believe it because it grants us the self-righteous luxury of continuing to *create* and *hate* our enemies.

I implore you, don't throw your book across the room just yet. Suspend disbelief with me for just a few more pages.

All the Signs, All the Wonders

Up to this point, everything Jesus did on earth, a person also did in His name. Let's unpack a few of these signs, wonders, and miracles.

Walking on water: Jesus did it and Peter did it. Admittedly, Peter wasn't too great at it, but he did it (Matthew 14:22-33).

Translation: Jesus did it and Philip did it. He was zapped from zip code to zip code in the blink of an eye in order to witness (Acts 8:39-40).

Multiplying food: Jesus did it and His disciples did it. And the result meant *thousands* were physically and spiritually fed (Matthew 14; Mark 8).

Healing the sick. Casting out demons. Raising the dead: Jesus gave His disciples power and authority to do all these things in His name. He said to them, "Heal the sick, raise the dead, cleanse the lepers, cast out demons. Freely you received, freely give" (Matthew 10:8).

Oh, but He doesn't stop there. Skip ahead to John's Gospel with me, just before the ascension. "Truly, truly, I say to you, he who believes in Me, the works that I do, he will do also; and greater works than these he will do; because I go to the Father. Whatever you ask in My name, that will I do, so that the Father may be glorified in the Son" (John 14:12-13). *Did you see that?* You have been given power and authority to do even greater things than Jesus displayed, so long as you do them in His name. He extends the same power and authority He gave His disciples to all who believe in Him. This is your current reality — your power and authority as a believer are a direct outpouring of your identity in Christ fully embraced.

Everything Jesus did, a person also did, except for *one* thing — the forgiveness of sins. And even now, grace is the one thing we still have a hard time with. We're far more comfortable declaring physical healing than extending radical grace. It's bizarre when you think about it. As Spirit-filled believers, we want all the signs, all the wonders. We want the supernatural "wow" factor, and we *think* we mean it when we cry out, "More, Lord!" But releasing forgiveness through the reckless love of God is the greatest supernatural gift Jesus imparts to us. We know it's true, because He saves His best gift for last.

After creation, we fall. After the resurrection, we are restored *to our original identity.* And out of that identity come power and authority in the spirit realm. Jesus already gave authority to cast out demons and disease before His death (Luke 9:1; Matthew 10:1), but it isn't until *after* the resurrection that He invites us to represent Him in *everything*, including His *grace*.

Grace Redefined

If you're like most people, anything that challenges your list of enemies is uncomfortable. *Lean in* to that refining discomfort. It hurts so good. And if you stay with me, you'll get a fresh revelation of God's character revealed in Jesus's own words. And when you do? It will change everything you thought you knew about grace and forgiveness. You see, your sin is erased by Christ alone — all you do is choose to come into agreement with Him by aligning yourself with the redemption of the cross. "He who was delivered over because of our transgressions, and was raised because of our justification" (Romans 4:24). When you withhold forgiveness, you fail to recognize the power of the cross, you misrepresent Christ, and the world remains blind to the love and grace of the Father.

The gospel of Jesus Christ is offensive to our post-Christian culture, and for good reason. It almost always comes down to *radical grace*. Grace that makes no sense by earthly standards. Grace we cannot possibly steward faithfully in our own strength.

You Already Have the Gift of Grace

The best part about God's gift of grace? You already have it. You already possess the power and authority to forgive sins in Jesus's name. If you're still wrestling with this truth, know you're not alone. You see, people *love* to scrutinize Jesus's theology. Religious leaders in His day often cried "Blasphemer!" in response to God's truth revealed in Jesus's words. And while we would never presume to be so *direct* with Jesus, refusing to believe the truth of His words cries out in silence the very same.

In Mark 2, we find a story of a paralyzed man I'm going to call Joe. (His name isn't really Joe, but trust me, giving him a name sounds so much nicer than "the paralytic.")

GRACE REDEFINED

Joe has some incredible friends who are ready to see him healed *right now*. So they do what anyone in Capernaum would do. They take him to a local meeting at Peter's mother-in-law's house to see Jesus. The problem is, it's *so packed* they can't even get in the door. So they come up with one of the most ridiculous ideas in Scripture. "Let's go *through the roof*," one of them says. And Joe's buddies think it's *brilliant*. They bust a hole in the roof of Peter's mother-in-law's house and proceed to lower Joe down into a crowd of people to get to Jesus.

Consider the pure insanity of this moment. A paralyzed man swinging from a gaping hole in the ceiling. Forget the Sunday School coloring page images of a neatly engineered operation with a room of welcoming faces. The scene is college-frat-boy level *crazy*, and you know Peter's mother-in-law has *got* to be *thrilled* about her new skylight. It's a bold move — reckless and desperate. But *what other option* do Joe's friends have?

Meanwhile, Joe never says a word. Maybe he was speechless from fear of falling. Maybe he didn't really want to be there. Maybe he didn't really believe Jesus could heal him. Who knows? But when Jesus sees *the faith of his friends* — his crazy, reckless, irresponsible friends — He says to Joe, "Son, you are forgiven." Did you read that carefully? Take a closer look. "And Jesus seeing *their faith* said to the paralytic, 'Son, your sins are forgiven'" (Mark 2:5, emphasis mine).

Meanwhile, the people in the room are having a religious fit — not because of the hole in the roof, but because Jesus has the audacity to think He has the power and authority to forgive sins. "Why does this man speak that way? He is blaspheming; who can forgive sins but God alone?" (Mark 2:7). Sound familiar? "Who can forgive sins

GRACE REDEFINED

but God alone?" *That's* where you heard it! From the mouths of religious zealots desperate to disprove Jesus's divinity and scrutinize His theology. Some things never change. Whether they hear His voice firsthand or read His words on a worn parchment page, the truth of the grace Jesus imparts can be hard to accept. But Jesus will never call us to a place we couldn't follow. It's not in His nature to set us up for failure.

In the Scriptures, Jesus most often refers to Himself as "Son of Man," focusing squarely on His humanness. And He insists the Son of Man can do *nothing* of Himself, that He can only *do* what He sees His Father do and *say* what He hears His Father say (John 5:19). Each and every time Jesus refers to Himself as Son of Man, He's revealing the full potential of every believer who is freed from sin and surrendered to the power of the Holy Spirit. I would like to suggest that Jesus — fully God, yet fully man — lived out the most *normal* Christian life in history. His day-to-day *intimacy* with God and *influence* with man is meant to be an attainable model for our present reality.

Jesus responds to their scrutiny in true Jesus form. "Which is easier," He asks, "to say to [Joe], 'Your sins are forgiven'; or to say, 'Get up, and pick up your pallet and walk'?" (Mark 2:8-9).

Then He brings it home.

"But so that you may know that the Son of Man has authority on earth to forgive sins," He said to [Joe], "I say to you, get up, pick up your pallet and go home" (vv. 10-11).

Jesus releases both healing *and forgiveness* to Joe — a man who never even *asked* for it — all in the same breath. "Son, your sins are forgiven." Does he have to say, "Get up and walk" for Joe to do it? Of course not. He says it to reinforce the full authority He has as Son of Man and to demonstrate the authority we are meant to emulate in the release of grace.

Everything Jesus did, a person also did. And *you* are invited to do it too. You have been given a gift of radical, unthinkable, supernatural grace, and you are uniquely suited to use that grace to help bring God's kingdom here and now.

Grace Redefined

It's a bold move to write a book on grace. And in doing so, I feel the need to define it — or *redefine it* — in the heart and mind of anyone reading this message. *What is grace*, really? It's not what you think. It's not a *thing*. It's not a *feeling*. It's a *person. Jesus Christ is the embodiment of grace.* He was and is grace, and what's more, He imparted it to all believers in the upper room that night (Luke 22:24-38).

Here's the big question about John 20:23, and it will change everything. Is Jesus *serious?* Was He joking? Was He giving us an option? We must deal with the ramifications of what it means for human relationships if He indeed meant for us to love our enemies. If we forgive others' sins, they're forgiven. If we retain them, they're retained. Does He mean that *literally* or as part of some unattainable religious ideal? Does He actually mean we are meant to demonstrate grace like God does and that if we don't, there are eternal consequences — for us and for the ones we won't forgive?

I don't know about you, but those red-letter words of Jesus are the ones I *really* take to heart, in full context, in light of how they were intended. After His resurrection,

GRACE REDEFINED

Jesus speaks plainly to His disciples — no metaphor, no analogy, no room for interpretation. So yes, Jesus is serious. God wants you to walk in His divine gift of radical grace. But God hasn't taken away your options. He won't twist your arm and make you do the righteous thing. Walking in this radical grace is a conscious decision you get to make. It's not a feeling, not an emotion; it's a choice. Not just a choice to forgive, but a choice to come into agreement with God about what He thinks of others.

Extending grace is an opportunity to come into agreement with the redeeming love of a God who keeps no record of wrongs and commands you to love your enemies — an opportunity that not only brings *freedom to you* but also gives them the opportunity of *an encounter* with Jesus Christ. At first it can feel like death. Surrender often does. But in time it becomes an outpouring of the radical grace you've received in your own life.

> *Do you struggle to* extend *grace and forgiveness?*
>
> *Do you struggle to* receive *grace and forgiveness?*

So many believers do. I do too. The truth is, we can't do anything in our own strength.

- We can't forgive in our own strength.
- We can't heal in our own strength.
- We can't cast out demons in our own strength.
- We can't even hold onto our faith in our own strength.

So why do we think we have to *strive* for grace when it's already been freely given? Thankfully, God loves to use the weakest, most unqualified people to bring His kingdom in ways only He could be responsible for.

If you're someone who struggles with offense and unforgiveness — for others or for yourself — God is ready to obliterate your disbelief through a fresh release of His radical grace.

COMING INTO AGREEMENT WITH GOD

Grace manifested in your own life is miraculously uncomplicated. It simply means coming into agreement with God about what He thinks of others and of you. Sounds easy, right? But how do you *know* if you're agreeing with God? Search your heart with these two critical questions:

1. *Is there anyone you hold an offense against?*

   Pause and search your heart for a moment. Do you have a "that person" in your life who you genuinely struggle to extend grace to?

2. *Is there anyone God wouldn't forgive?*

   Do you hold an offense against someone *even* God wouldn't hold? Would God forgive your "that person?"

Maybe "that person" came to mind immediately. Your jerk coworker. Your ex. That guy who flipped you off in traffic this morning. Maybe even an authority figure or political leader came to mind.

Jesus lays it out clearly in the seventh line of the Lord's Prayer: "And forgive us our debts, as we also have forgiven our debtors" (Matthew 6:12). The assumption here is that you *have forgiven*. This phrase is the foundation of what it

Grace Redefined

means to come into agreement with God, and it clearly displays the kind of grace He wants you to have.

Enemy: A False Construct

Your "that person" may be someone you consider an enemy. If this is true (even if you'd never say it aloud), you are missing out on an opportunity to live out the fullness of grace God has given you. "Enemy" is, in fact, a false mental construct created by people carrying offense at the transgressions of another. The earthy label gives us a perceived license to hate, a right to withhold grace, and a justification to carry offense *to the death* like a badge of honor. But the truth is, *nobody* can be your enemy without your permission.

King David marvels at how the Lord prepares a table before him in the presence of his enemies (Psalm 23:5). Why would God do such a thing? It's simple. So you can be a living invitation for your "enemy" to realize his true identity... and become your brother. "I say to you who hear, love your enemies, do good to those who hate you, bless those who curse you, pray for those who mistreat you" (Luke 6:27-28). When Jesus implores us to love our enemies, He is *just as serious* as when He releases the authority to forgive sins in the upper room. Both concepts, equally radical, pierce us to the core. It's a reckless call to unity and oneness that simply doesn't make sense in this world. When you walk in your true identity in Christ, you won't be able to see people as enemies, but as broken beings who desperately need to encounter the God of grace. When all else fails, love truly wins, for God is love.

But perhaps this isn't you. Maybe you're not the one who has been wronged. Maybe you're the one who has sinned against another and against God, and you're stuck

GRACE REDEFINED

in a cycle of sin and shame. The only thing more difficult than forgiving *someone else* is forgiving *yourself*. But here's the funny thing about grace. There's a divine order to it, and it differentiates between grace as a gift and grace as a reward. Grace starts as a gift from the Father, released to us through Jesus Christ, not *because* we earned it, but *before* we could even know to ask for it. The grace we're called to extend to others through the forgiveness of sins isn't something we do to earn God's grace in return. It's something we do as a natural overflow of the radical grace we've already received.

You cannot give away what you have first not received. You must *receive* grace as a gift before you can *give* it. And you must *give* grace as an overflow of that gift before you can *receive* grace as a reward from God. The best way to move toward forgiving yourself is to extend the grace you've been given to someone who doesn't deserve it.

Have you received God's gift of radical grace, released through Jesus Christ and imparted by the Holy Spirit? Would you like to?

ONE WORD OF WARNING

A common phrase you hear in church before an offering goes something like this: "Give and it will be given to you" (Luke 6:38). Ready for a shocking revelation? This passage has *nothing* to do with money and *everything* to do with grace! I'm all for radical generosity in our giving, but this is yet another instance where context is so very important.

If Jesus *was* serious when He imparted grace (John 20:23), what does that mean for our lives?

- We would have to *take inventory* on how much grace we're releasing.

GRACE REDEFINED

- We would have to *take an honest look* at how much grace we're receiving.
- We would have to *take responsibility* for a world that doesn't know grace is within reach.

If Jesus *wasn't* serious, we can assume it's not within our power to forgive sins. And if that's true, so is the following: Jesus may forgive you, but I don't have to. If you're not careful, you can justify offense and unforgiveness in your own heart by leaving grace up to God. But the challenge of John 20:23 is this: Jesus is calling all believers to put on display the amount of grace we believe God is giving, not just to the world, but to ourselves. "Forgive us our debts, as we also have forgiven our debtors." In case you're confused, let's break that down for a moment.

If you don't *forgive, your Father* won't *forgive you.*

If you do *forgive, your Father* will *forgive you.*

It sounds like a threat, but it's actually an incredibly powerful tool in unleashing the power of God's grace gift in your life. The best part? You don't have to figure it out. Like any other sign or wonder, grace isn't something for you to boast in or try to own in your flesh. God is the one who heals, the one who restores, the one who forgives. He just chooses to invite us into what He's up to by giving us power and authority as His children. We are invited to *personally* usher in the kingdom of God through His manifest grace, not because our salvation is dependent upon it, but because we're His kids!

If you have received Christ as your Lord and Savior, you have been adopted into God's family. It's unlike any earthly adoption you've ever heard of. Kingdom adoption

GRACE REDEFINED

is an awakening to who you really are in Christ — a beloved son or daughter of the King by new birthright! And out of that new identity in Christ, we learn to be more like our Abba, our Father — to look like Him, act like Him, and extend grace and forgiveness like Him. God loves you so much, He wants you to have an opportunity to get in on the goodness of His radical grace. It's just what you do as part of His family.

God's grace sounds reckless by the world's standards. *And it is.* But it's no more than what you've already been given. God wants you focused on Him in this learning process, not on your own willingness to forgive (or lack thereof). As always, His strength is made perfect in your weakness. And from that place of humility, of coming into agreement with God, you begin to scratch the surface of what radical grace unleashed *really* looks like.

GRACE REFLECTIONS

1. Do you struggle to extend grace to others? Why or why not?
2. Do you struggle to receive grace from others? Why or why not?
3. After reading John 20:23, do you believe Jesus was serious about extending grace? If not, why not? If so, what do His words mean for your life right now?

2 Grace Received

For it is in giving that we receive; it is in pardoning that we are pardoned; it is in dying that we are born to eternal life.
— *Saint Francis of Assisi*

Grace Received

Grace in the Overflow

In the early stages of this book, my coauthor, Brit, and I had revelation about manifest grace that not only shifted this book's outline, it also took striving out of the grace equation for anyone willing to read it. I was preaching a portion of this grace message at a conference in southeast Ohio, and Brit was in the audience listening for any fresh revelation God might have in the message. I finished speaking, and she made her way through the crowd to meet me down front.

"We have it backward in the outline," she said, in a moment of breakthrough. At this point, the first four chapters of part 1, "The Grace Message," were ordered as follows:

1. Grace Redefined,
2. Grace Released,
3. Grace Received, and
4. Grace of God.

"Bill, the reason it's so hard for people to *release* God's grace is because they haven't fully *received* it yet," she insisted. "And the reason they haven't fully *received* it is because they don't know they *already have it!*"

Understanding that you need to receive God's grace before releasing it will change everything for you as you dive deeper into the grace learning process. You learned in the last chapter that God has already given you the gift of His grace. It's yours! Do you believe it yet? In this chapter, we'll cover the importance of really *receiving* that grace gift you've been given — not by trying harder to earn it or striving to release it in your own strength, but by learning to rest in the loving arms of your gracious heavenly Father.

GRACE RECEIVED

Jesus was completely serious when He released the gift of grace to His disciples (John 20:23), but He intends for us to extend grace to others *as an overflow* of the grace we have received from Him.

> *The kind of reckless grace we're called to release as believers only works in the overflow — as a fresh outpouring of the grace we are willing to receive.*

Let's explore the power of the grace at our fingertips, ripe and ready for the harvest.

God's grace isn't something you can manifest out of your own strength, so please don't try. As with all spiritual gifts, you can't earn God's grace. You don't deserve it. It makes no logical, earthly sense. And because we struggle to understand God's grace, we build up barriers to receiving it. Our obedience in releasing grace becomes contingent upon our full understanding of God's grace, leaving us stuck in a cycle of sin, guilt, shame, and unforgiveness. From that broken place, we keep ourselves at arm's length (or longer) from a God who desperately wants to lavish His grace upon us and others. It doesn't have to be this way. Let's go back to basics for a moment.

"For God so loved the world, that He gave His only begotten Son, that whoever believes in Him shall not perish, but have eternal life" (John 3:16). These are some of the most potent, transformative, highly-quoted words in Scripture, and it's easy to see why. They are *living proof* of God's intentions when He gave us the gift of grace through our salvation. God gave *everything* to have us with Him for all eternity. He gave His only begotten Son, Jesus, as a perfect sacrifice, while we were *still sinners*. Why would God do this, knowing full well that many would reject His gift?

Grace Received

What motivation did He have in this move of reckless grace?

Love. God *always* starts with love.

The first four words in verse 16, "For God so loved," are stacked with precision by John in hopes that we would get a clear picture of how God initiates grace. God loved us *first*, which is why He sent Jesus to the depths of hell and back again to defeat sin and death and give us eternal life. And that salvation would be enough on its own . . . but there's more. (Of course there is. This *is* God we're talking about.) Look at the next two verses. "For God did not send the Son into the world to judge the world, but that the world might be saved through Him. He who believes in Him is not judged; he who does not believe has been judged already, because he has not believed in the name of the only begotten Son of God" (John 3:17-18).

Did you catch that? If you believe in Jesus, you're not judged. You're free. If you don't believe in Jesus, you're *still* not judged. Why? Because you're *already* guilty, dead in your sin. And by not believing in the name of Jesus, you're just choosing to *stay* guilty. He wants to bring you from death to life eternal, and you're saying no thanks to the greatest gift you will ever be offered. That's not what you want, right?

Receiving God's grace is a fourfold agreement:

1. receiving what Jesus has done *for you*,
2. receiving what Jesus has done *to you*,
3. receiving what Jesus has done *in you*, and
4. receiving what Jesus will do *as you*.

What He did *for you* is covered in John 3:16. Jesus *saved* you! He *rescued* you from sin and death. He *erased* your sin.

He initiated grace and *forgave* you. And that would have been enough! But there's *more*. What He did *to you* is covered (vv. 17-18). Jesus *restored* you! He made you innocent and blameless in God's sight. Your identity is now and will forever be "beloved child of God." He reconciled you to Himself, making you *the home* for His presence and the manifest expression of His love, mercy, and grace to the world. Oh, but there's more. What He has done to you has the power to transform your mind, heart, body, spirit, and will. This is the power of Christ *in you*, the hope of glory. And with the power of Christ in you, He is able to move *as you;* He will move *through you* as an earthen vessel to release His reckless grace.

Do you see the magnitude of this four-part agreement? Jesus Christ doesn't just offer you salvation, He invites you to come home into the throne room as a coheir with Christ, our redeemer. To receive this grace, *respond* with an emphatic *yes!* and choose to *believe* in the wonderful, beautiful, powerful name of Jesus. It may take some time for your head to catch up with your heart in this true belief, but there's grace to cover you in the waiting.

So Who Condemns Us?

"In the beginning was the Word, and the Word was with God, and the Word was God" (John 1:1). John gets straight to the point, doesn't he? In the account of Jesus's life as written by the apostle John, or "that disciple whom Jesus loved" as he liked to call himself, all Jesus has to do is say the word and it's *done*. Healing, forgiveness, grace, love, mercy, freedom, restoration, resurrection . . . the list goes on. As effortlessly as God spoke creation into existence, so does Jesus speak into being the fullness of God's grace to mankind. In John's Gospel, Jesus simultaneously erases the

Grace Received

history of the fall (Genesis 3) and invites us to reclaim our original identity as God's image bearers, beloved sons and daughters of the King of heaven, all by the power of His spoken Word.

In his writing, John is determined to shift our minds away from the pain of the fall and toward the righteousness we believers have in Christ Jesus. His narrative positioning proves that he wants you to know how truly loved you are by God and how much grace you've really been given. A few chapters in, he shows Jesus beginning to unpack the raw truth about condemnation. And in true Jesus form, it's not what anyone is expecting to hear. "Not even the Father judges anyone, but He has given all judgment to the Son" (John 5:22). Interesting, isn't it? Jesus is essentially saying, *God's not judging you, He delegated that to Me.* But when Jesus elaborates on the topic of judgment (John 12), it starts to get *wild*. "If anyone hears My sayings and does not keep them, I do not judge him; for I did not come to judge the world, but to save the world" (v. 47). This is a *radical* assertion of grace. Jesus is basically saying, *Hey, even if you don't do what I say, even if you don't believe what I say, I'm still not judging you. Why? Because that's not why I'm here. I came to save you!*

Okay, back up.

The Father isn't judging you (John 5:22). Jesus isn't judging you (John 12:47). Wait a minute. So who is judging? Jesus challenges our assumptions about the judgement against us (back in John 5:45), creating an awareness of our own self-inflicted condemnation. "Do not think that I will accuse you before the Father; the one who accuses you is Moses, in whom you have set your hope." He doesn't say these words to dishonor Moses by labeling him an accuser; instead, He uses it as an opportunity to

GRACE RECEIVED

invite to shift our eyes from the old covenant, one of condemnation, to a new covenant in Him — one of grace.

So the Father isn't judging you. Jesus isn't judging you. Moses and the law can't judge you. You don't even get to judge yourself (v. 45). Again, who is judging? In verse 48, Jesus finally gives us the answer. "He who rejects Me and does not receive My sayings, has one who judges him; the word I spoke is what will judge him at the last day" (John 12:48). As we wonder *who* is judging us, we're asking the wrong question. It's not some*one* who will judge us, it's some*thing*. It's the Word Jesus spoke. Whether or not we are obedient to the Word is what we will be held to account for on the last day. Why is this differentiation important? Because it allows you to see Jesus Christ for who He really is, and yourself for who you really are in Him.

Jesus didn't come into the world to whip you into shape and impose salvation on you. He didn't come with a list of demands or an easy five-step plan for you to earn your righteousness before God. He came to invite you into a personal relationship with Himself — one that would change you forever. Jesus Christ came to restore the original identity you were given at creation so that you can choose obedience to the Word He speaks, not out of fear or obligation, but as a *joyful response* to the grace He extends. Jesus paid it all so you could be reconciled to the Father and brought into the throne room of grace as the royalty you are. And as you might have guessed, there's *still more*. "For I did not speak on My own initiative, but the Father Himself who sent Me has given Me a commandment as to what to say and what to speak" (John 12:49).

GRACE RECEIVED

If we're honest, we know we *deserve* judgment, "for all have sinned and fall short of the glory of God, being justified as a gift by His grace through the redemption which is in Christ Jesus" (Romans 3:23-24). Humanity was condemned at the fall and now we're born with a bent toward sin. Before we receive Christ, we're already judged guilty by the law. Sadly, spiritual leaders leverage this old sin and shame to guilt you into a works-based theology, probably because they, too, have yet to receive God's gift of grace in full. But I won't spend any more time trying to convince you of your sin. I'm much more interested in convincing you of your righteousness in Jesus Christ. The Father and the Son both have the authority to condemn you. But guess what? *They choose not to!* God's not judging us, and Jesus isn't judging us either. Instead, we will be held to account on the last day, not by Jesus Himself, but by the truth of the Word He spoke and our willingness to be obedient to it.

Is your brain scrambled yet? Let's take it one level deeper. This part will *wreck you* in the best kind of way.

Jesus only *says* and *does* what His Father commands. In other words, the Word He spoke is God's commandment — the same Word that will one day judge us. So what is God's commandment? What's the Word He spoke? The *same word* that will one day judge us? "I know that His commandment is eternal life; therefore the things I speak, I speak just as the Father has told Me" (John 12:50). "Eternal life!" I kid you not, it's right there in John's Gospel. His commandment is our commission: to know the Father, the one true God, and Jesus Christ whom He sent (John 17:3). Eternal life has *already* been given to us; we just have to say yes! You can't make this stuff up. God is good, so, so good. He's *even better* than you think He is.

Grace Received

A dear friend of mine, Dr. William Lewis, speaks the following words over people on a regular basis. They are personal to his heart, and there is so much life pouring out of them.

> *Who is in a position to condemn you? Only Jesus. And yet Jesus died for you. Jesus rose for you. And even now, Jesus sits at the right hand of the Father interceding on your behalf. As you receive the love and grace of Jesus, the past, with all of its mistakes, is gone. You are forgiven, made new and innocent in Christ.*

Believe this good news, friend. Receive His reckless grace and be at peace. You can't earn it, so please, *stop trying so hard*. Just say yes! Let His goodness and mercy transform your heart, your mind, your body, your soul, your will, and your *actions* as you learn to release grace as Jesus did — in the overflow of grace received.

Forgiving Yourself in the Light of Grace

The most common barrier to receiving God's gift of grace is *you*. You may *think* you believe God gives you grace, mercy, and forgiveness. You may respond with a tentative yes to Jesus and profess to believe in His name. You may even be willing to make the case *intellectually* for grace to manifest in your own life. But somewhere deep down, you still wonder . . . *Am I really forgiven?* Whether this is a question you've pondered about yourself or heard from another, the truth about grace received will give you the freedom you need to release it.

Let me tell you a story about my friend Frank. I met him years ago on a beach in Kihei, Maui, where my team

Grace Received

did regular ministry outreaches. Frank's wit and charm were inviting. A professed agnostic, Frank was a retired professor of philosophy at a west coast university. Very set in his ways, he wasn't about to delegitimize his life's convictions to make a radical shift in his later years. So when it came to the topic of Jesus, we argued. A lot.

One week, my ministry team got a fresh dose of grace through a revelation of compassion. We realized God used *compassion* to move Jesus to release healing and deliverance. We began to see it in Scripture time and again. "Jesus moved with compassion . . ." and then, *suddenly*, a miracle happened. So together we opened our hearts to allow the compassion that moved Jesus to move us as well.

A few days later, I was back in Kihei with a ministry team and we ran into Frank. He smiled and greeted us warmly, and we began to talk. It wasn't our usual argument but a healthy dialogue on the judgmental way Christians *look at* and are *viewed by* the world. God broke my heart for Frank. For the first time, I saw him through God's lens, and I came into agreement with what God said about him. God moved me with a supernatural compassion to do something bold, so I placed my hand on his shoulder and made a declaration over him.

"Frank, no matter what your view of Jesus Christ and His church, this is the truth: All of your sins have been forgiven."

Shocked, he said with doubt in his voice, "Well that would be a nice idea if it were true but . . ."

"No," I replied. "I'm absolutely serious when *I declare* to you that all of your sins are forgiven." I was moved by compassion, and the declarations started spilling out of my mouth in Spirit-filled waves. They crashed into his soul like

GRACE RECEIVED

the very waves upon the rocks where we sat, and I could feel it.

"*I declare* to you that Jesus didn't ask your permission to erase your sins. He just *did it* when He died for you, once and for all. Now, when Father God looks at you, He looks through the filter of the blood of His Son, Jesus Christ. And because of that blood, you are absolutely free from sin, guilt, and shame.

"*I declare* to you that your past has not disqualified you from a future of encounters with Christ and that you can know at this moment that you are absolutely clean." Then I asked him a question that changed the course of his future. "Frank, do you *believe* what I'm saying?"

He began to weep and said, "I don't know why, I don't understand how, but I've never felt like this in all my life." Frank walked into true freedom and began a relationship with Jesus Christ that very day. And it all came about not through a persuasive argument but through a movement of compassion, the same compassion God used to move Jesus to action on earth. Frank, experiencing the power of forgiveness released through a supernatural declaration of grace, was finally able to forgive himself.

I understand the theological tweaking you might be feeling right now, because I felt it too. How could this happen when Frank did nothing but believe? How could I say he "got saved" without his saying the sinner's prayer? How could I even have the confidence that what I declared was enough to get him into heaven? I confess, I wrestled with each one of these thoughts. But Frank's conversion was genuine and the fruit of it remained.

Frank passed away not long after, but I have full confidence in his eternal destination. I watched a heart

GRACE RECEIVED

align with the power of the resurrection and knew that, as much as a man can believe in the power of Jesus to be Savior and Lord, Frank believed.

Forgiving yourself is one of the hardest things you'll ever do. Maybe you picked up this book for strategies to help you forgive others, and we'll talk more about that in chapter 3, "Releasing Grace," but *forgiving yourself* is a critical part of *receiving* the fullness of God's grace, which is the first step toward being able to release grace toward others. You may be thinking, *But Bill, you don't know what I've done. And if you did, you'd understand why I can't forgive myself.* Friend, whether you've sinned against God, sinned against a brother or sister — or even sinned against yourself — there is no sin so great that God won't forgive it. And if there's no sin God won't forgive, there is no sin for you to hold against yourself.

This is where Satan's voice can get really loud. The enemy of your soul wants you to believe that forgiving yourself is more shameful than carrying the burden as penance. He lies! This demonic line of thinking holds you in bondage, ashamed of your shame. What's worse, it keeps you separated from God. If you hear this in your mind or from another person, dismiss it immediately.

When you choose not to forgive yourself, you're choosing not to come into agreement with God. In refusing to forgive yourself, you're refusing God's grace as well. Saying to yourself you're not forgiven is calling God a liar. You may think it's humble to punish and withhold grace from yourself. Don't be deceived. It's actually coming from a secret place of pride. It shows you think you know better than God and that His ways are not best. God wants you to walk in the light of the freedom He gave you. Forgiving yourself is part of coming into agreement with

GRACE RECEIVED

what God says about you. He says you're forgiven — absolutely free from sin, guilt, and shame. Who are you to say otherwise? The world may judge you for what you've done, but you need to *know* that you *know* that you *know* the truth: you are forgiven! Your Father in heaven calls you "beloved child." Nothing can separate you from His love (Romans 8:38-39). And He loves you so much, He gave everything to have you back again. God's opinion of you is the only one that matters in the end. God's Word says your sin and death are defeated. They hold no power over you. You're in Christ and He's in you! Jesus's final word on the cross says it sure enough: "It is finished!" (John 19:30).

To access the reckless grace of Christ, you must:

1. believe it,
2. receive it,
3. release it, and
4. repeat.

As finite beings, we overcomplicate this process, striving to release grace before we've really received it, striving again on the repeat. We'll dig deeper into this process later on. What you need to know now is that however nonlinear your journey into the fullness of God's grace, there will come a day when you realize the truth: you can't give away what you don't really believe you have.

As I share this grace message with you, I fully submit to the authority of Scripture, and I encourage you to do the same. I am unapologetically unashamed in rebuking religious practices that keep you in chains. I pray that you will surrender all fear and pride, receive God's grace, and receive the gift of grace Jesus released (in John 20:23). May

Grace Received

you walk in the light of the reckless grace you've been given and be moved with compassion to give it away.

Grace Reflections

1. Is there anything you struggle to forgive yourself for?
2. Do you really believe all your sins are forgiven by God? Why or why not?
3. Will you receive the gift of grace God has already given you through the finished work of Jesus Christ?

3 Grace Released

Lord, how often shall my brother sin against me and I forgive him? Up to seven times? — Matthew 18:21

GRACE RELEASED

PETER PUTS GRACE IN A BOX

Simon Peter, one of the twelve, was an outspoken, strong-willed, fiercely passionate disciple and one of Jesus's closest friends. Peter is one of my favorite disciples because he's so raw, so real, so imperfect. He's *proof* that God can take a hotheaded serial sinner and transform him into a saint through reckless grace. Grace received in Peter's life moved him with compassion to *release it* by living out the rest of his days for Jesus and, ultimately, giving his life for Christ.

Let's dive into Matthew 18, starting in verse 15. Jesus is in the middle of a teaching on grace and forgiveness. Even if you've read this chapter many times before, you will see it with fresh eyes in light of grace *redefined* in your mind and *received* in your heart. Here's a little context for the conversation: Jesus is with His disciples in Capernaum, walking them through the basics of everybody's *favorite* topic: church discipline! He lays down some rules for helping to restore a person who sins. (Yes, in case you missed that last time you worked through the Gospels: *restoring* our brothers and sisters is an important part of our responsibilities as believers. This restoration comes from a place of grace and forgiveness, not judgment or condemnation.) Jesus is encouraging His disciples to work out their disagreements and offenses instead of holding onto them, explaining the process for involving others, and even the church, if necessary. They're/we're not only called to restore them, but to do so *gently* (Galatians 6:1). It's such a new concept for this crowd. The disciples are listening intently, trying to wrap their heads around it.

Now Peter, hoping to come off *especially* benevolent in front of his brothers, asks a bold clarifying question in light of the law-abiding, eye-for-an-eye culture of the day. "Lord, how often shall my brother sin against me and I forgive him?" (I'm sure he pauses for dramatic impact.) "Up to *seven times?*"

If facepalms were a thing in that day, I imagine Jesus doing one right here. Peter doesn't get it. But in his defense, even at risk of rebuke, the question is worth asking. In those days, even the most God-honoring Jewish rabbis would suggest forgiving an offense no more than *three times* (Amos 1:3), because grace *has* to have limits, right? Lest we be enablers. . . .

Interestingly, there's some ambiguity in the Greek covering Jesus's answer to Peter's bold question. Let's take a look at two common translations, the New International Version (NIV) and the New American Standard Bible (NASB).

> Jesus answered, "I tell you, not seven times, but *seventy-seven* times."
> — Matthew 18:22 (NIV)

> Jesus said to him, "I do not say to you, up to seven times, but up to *seventy times seven.*"
> — Matthew 18:22 (NASB)

I'm not here to debate the accuracy of these translations, but in my opinion, this disputed numerical uncertainty only reinforces the point of Jesus's reply. Whether He intended for Peter to hear *seventy-seven* times or *four hundred and ninety* times is irrelevant, because He may as well have said *seventy-seven million* times! *Jesus is inviting Peter and all believers to be willing to* out-grace *an offense.* In this high-challenge exchange, Jesus is emphasizing that His grace has no limits.

GRACE RELEASED

So why should yours? Jesus wants your grace giving to overcome others' ability to offend you — not to empower their sin, but to free you *and* them from it!

The irony of this challenge comes full circle for Peter surrounding Christ's death and resurrection. Just as Jesus predicted (Matthew 26:34), Peter denies Jesus *three times* — a number no rabbi would be willing to extend grace beyond, except for one. After all, Jesus is no ordinary rabbi. Do you remember what Jesus had claimed He would do to those who denied Him before men? He stated emphatically that He would deny the deniers before His Father (Matthew 10:33). Yet Peter denies Jesus three times and Jesus chooses to redeem him instead. Do you find it difficult to believe that God, the same God who commands us to love our enemies, would do the same?

As the disciples finish breakfast with the resurrected Christ on the shore of the Sea of Galilee (John 21), Jesus demonstrates an out-of-the-box grace Peter isn't expecting. He turns the tables with a question for Peter. "Simon, son of John, do you love Me more than these?" (John 21:15). He doesn't just ask it once. He doesn't ask it twice. He asks it *three times*. Not only that — Jesus calls him by his old name, Simon, son of John, instead of Peter, the new name Jesus had given him as "the rock" on which His church would be built. *Ouch.* This third "Do you love Me?" ask really stings, as Peter's guilt and shame over his three denials begin to rise up in the midst of an otherwise joyous moment. He recalls his sin, the lies of betrayal he *knows* he doesn't deserve grace for. He's *got* to be sweating bullets, wondering if Jesus *really* meant what He said about forgiveness back in Capernaum.

Now if Jesus were anyone *other than* Jesus, He might sit there for a bit, *reveling* in His superiority. And He would have every right by earthly standards. Three betrayals would be difficult for any human to endure, even for the Son of Man. Thankfully for Peter – and for us – *Jesus is Jesus*, and He has a much greater purpose in mind when He asks, "Do you love Me?" That purpose can get a little lost in translation, so let's go back to the Greek.

The Greek word "love" loses power when translated into English. You see, the Bible contains *four* ancient words for love in the original Greek:

1. *Philia (φιλία)* – meaning "friendship" or brotherly love (Strong's, "philia"),

2. *Storge (στοργή)* – meaning reciprocally affectionate, "familial" or "parental" love (Strong's, "philostorgos"),

3. *Eros (ἔρως)* – meaning "erotic" or sexual love (Strong's, "phaneros"), and

4. *Agape (ἀγάπη)* – meaning "love of God" or unconditional love (Strong's "agape").

The original text shows each time Jesus asks this famous "Do you love me?" question of Peter: He uses the Greek word *agape* for love – a word that doesn't just mean "love" but "unconditional love," regardless of circumstance. Here's the interesting part. The first two times Jesus asks him, Peter replies, "Yes, Lord; You know that I love You." Except when Peter says "love," he doesn't reply with the same *agape* word for love, but *phileo* – a verb conjugation of the Greek word *philia* that translates to mean "brotherly love." Imagine asking a friend, "Do you love me unconditionally, no matter what?" and having him respond, "Yeah, sure, you know I love you, brother." Jesus is inviting Peter to see that he must love and forgive unconditionally in order to manifest a faithful release of God's grace.

The word "unconditionally" as an adverb is defined as "without conditions or limits." Do you know how to *love* like that? Do you know how to *forgive* like that? Do you know how to *extend grace* like that? *Would you like to?* If your answer is yes, then Jesus's response to you will mirror the one He gave Peter: "Tend My sheep" (v. 17). Now to many of us, this sounds a little like a demotion, doesn't it? Far from it! Jesus is the Good Shepherd, right? Not a literal sheep herder, but the One who shepherds all believers and calls them to unity. He is willing to leave behind ninety-nine other obedient sheep to chase down one lambkin who went astray in a fit of disobedience. By our earthly standards, it's reckless. Why risk the ninety-nine for one? But by kingdom standards, it's the only way to go. Jesus ransomed us. He bought back our freedom with His life, and He still would have done it even if you were the only one who needed saving.

As a disciple of Jesus Christ, an adopted son or daughter of the King of heaven, you are both commissioned and qualified to release that same reckless grace and forgiveness, stopping at nothing to rescue the ones and bring them home again in Jesus's name. You've been invited to join the family business!

When Jesus invites Peter to tend His sheep *three times*, He is releasing grace — forgiving his three betrayals and restoring him in full — as "the rock" on which He'll build His church. Jesus erases his betrayals and makes Peter the very first pope to shepherd all believers after the ascension. Peter responds by giving every remaining moment he spends on earth to Jesus, laying the foundation for the freedoms in Christ we enjoy today. And how could Peter respond in any way, other than to make Jesus Lord over his entire life? He deserved *death* for his transgressions, but instead he received *grace* that lifted him into a position of high honor without ever *asking* Jesus for forgiveness! That's what the limitless, unthinkable, reckless grace of our God really looks like. That *same grace* now lives *within you* because of Jesus's grace gift released (in John 20:23). It's yours! Receive it in full, and release it, in Jesus's name.

EVEN DEATH WON'T SATISFY

The sobering thing is, the *justice* you seek will not bring the peace you hope for. Years ago, I was privileged to minister to a family invited to witness the execution of their son's murderer. They chose to attend, as many seeking justice for a loved one might. And despite witnessing earthly justice come down on a man who deserved death for what he had done, witnessing his death didn't take away the pain of losing their son. As they took justice into their own hands by witnessing the execution, they partnered with a spirit of earthly justice and put their hope in a punishment that was anything but divine retribution. Weeks later, they couldn't comprehend why they were still brokenhearted, bitter, and angry *at a dead man*. And when you can't even bring yourself to forgive a dead man, you know unforgiveness has a stronghold on your heart. This is what bondage looks like.

Our hearts were made to crave justice; we're wired for it as part of our divine DNA. The problem with earthly justice, as this family discovered, is that it never delivers God's peace. The old covenant eye-for-an-eye mentality just doesn't satisfy the way we wish it would. Even when wrongdoers get *exactly* what they deserve for what they've done, our hearts remain broken. We want justice. But it's

GRACE RELEASED

not ours to lay down. Instead, we're given a much harder, but far more healing, responsibility in light of a world as desperate for grace as we are — *forgiveness*. When we act from a place of judgment, it manifests separation from God. Grace, on the other hand, brings us back into reconciled union with Him.

> If anyone is in Christ, he is a new creature; the old things passed away; behold, new things have come. Now all these things are from God, who reconciled us to Himself through Christ and gave us the ministry of reconciliation, namely, that God was in Christ reconciling the world to Himself, not counting their trespasses against them, and He has committed to us the word of reconciliation.
>
> — 2 Corinthians 5:17–19

Grace manifests the union of reconciliation and restoration that Christ freely gave us in His finished work on the cross. God in Christ is reconciling us to Himself by not counting our trespasses against us. And now He has committed to us that same ministry of reconciliation.

> Therefore, we are ambassadors for Christ, as though God were making an appeal through us; we beg you on behalf of Christ, be reconciled to God. He made Him who knew no sin to be sin on our behalf, so that we might become the righteousness of God in Him.
>
> — vv. 20–21

It's such good news, isn't it? But the sobering reality of God's gift of reckless grace is this:

If the world doesn't know it's loved, forgiven, and filled with glory, it's not God's fault. It's ours.

GRACE RELEASED

Jesus gives us stewardship of His grace when He releases it over His disciples (in John 20:23). Be as radical or restrained as you want with this gift, but if you do what He calls and empowers you to do, you will set others free, just as Jesus did. The tangible release of God's grace over humanity is quite possibly the greatest evangelistic tool the church has never used. So consider this for a moment: *How much grace do you want to experience?* Grace has already been given to you as a gift. It's *yours*. I'm hoping by this point you've chosen to receive the gift, and all the power and authority that comes with it, because once you *truly* receive God's reckless grace, it's darn near impossible not to give away! Releasing that grace in the overflow becomes not only your *right* as a child of God, but your *responsibility* as a coheir to the kingdom of heaven with Jesus Christ. This is the magnitude of the gift you carry!

I'd be remiss if I didn't speak to the intensely practical benefits of releasing grace and forgiveness of sins in Jesus's name. Even secular psychologists will tell you that forgiveness is a powerful part of the solution to mental and emotional disorders. But it's not just *your* mental, emotional, physical, and spiritual health that's at stake. We're talking about a generation of believers poised for a grace revolution if we would dare to forgive like Jesus did — *recklessly*.

You may be wrestling with the word *reckless*, thinking, *God's not reckless, Bill! Why do you keep saying that?* If Scripture has taught us anything, it's that reckless grace brings about radical transformation in the hearts, minds, and lives of the most unlikely people. But I promise you this: you won't experience grace that defies logic, knows no limits, and would go to the ends of the earth to bring you back to the flock again until you *receive* and *release* the radical, relentless, *reckless* grace of God. And once you do, you will be able to fully embrace your role as a faithful steward of this reckless grace released in and through you.

Ushering in the fullness of God's grace is so much greater than our minds can comprehend. We may never fully grasp it. But I plan on spending the rest of my days learning more about how to extend grace, no matter the consequences.

But someone offended me!
I know. Release grace anyway.

But what he's doing is wrong!
It is. Release grace anyway.

But I'm not ready to forgive!
That's okay. Release grace anyway.

Do you see a theme here? *God is* anything but *withholding when it comes to grace.* He initiates. He doesn't write sinners off until their behavior changes. He doesn't hold back until He feels "ready" to forgive. And more often than not, He doesn't even wait until the offender is repentant! He *initiates* with grace. You see, God sees repentance as a direct *result* of His grace, not a formal *prerequisite* for it. It makes no earthly sense, but as believers, we're no longer confined to the grace limits of this world.

A WELL OF GRACE THAT NEVER RUNS DRY

Reckless grace means being willing to position your heart toward forgiveness, no matter how grave the offense. It means surrendering to the grace gift you have received and overflowing in it out of the sheer joy of possessing it. What it doesn't mean is giving a pass to someone who wrongs you. It doesn't mean enduring abuse or refusing to stand up for the powerless. It does not, in any way, excuse their

GRACE RELEASED

behavior. Instead, grace and forgiveness call offenders out with some of the sweetest words ever spoken, "I do not condemn you, either. Go. From now on sin no more: (John 8:11).

Some of you may be wondering why I'm handing out licenses to sin. I *assure* you that's not the case. (I'd never *hand out* licenses to sin; *I'd sell them!*) All joking aside, this reckless approach to grace is not something I've created to enable sin. It's something Jesus released to *defeat it.* Don't believe me? Ask the Samaritan woman at Jacob's well (John 4). She'll tell you what reckless grace looks like. It looks like Jesus risking His reputation as a rabbi and a Jew to even speak to her. After all, she's a Samaritan, and a *woman* at that. But Jesus not only *speaks* to her, He asks her for a drink!

Of course she's skeptical. Who wouldn't be? She gives Him a funny look and begins to protest. But Jesus isn't having it. "If you knew the gift of God, and who it is who says to you, 'Give Me a drink,' you would have asked Him, and He would have given you living water" (John 4:10).

The NASB is my go-to translation, but I love the way Eugene Peterson puts this passage in The Message. It states Jesus's intentions toward grace with clear authenticity. "If you knew the generosity of God and who I am, you would be asking *me* for a drink, and I would give you fresh, living water" (John 4:10 MSG).

Scandalous, isn't it? Jaws dropping all around, no doubt. Even the Samaritan woman is a little offended. *Seriously, dude? Who do you think you are? You don't even have a bucket, and you think you're better than Jacob!* (In case you're wondering, yes, that's my personal interpretation of verses 11 and 12.) Jesus goes on. "Everyone who drinks of this

GRACE RELEASED

water will thirst again; but whoever drinks of the water that I will give him shall never thirst; but the water that I will give him will become in him a well of water springing up to eternal life" (John 4:13-14). And now she's intrigued. *Never thirst again?* And here she is, lugging jar after jar of water, all day every day. Even if it's for all the wrong reasons, though, she wants some of *that* water. So she does exactly what Jesus wants her to do — she asks Him for it!

The concept of *living water* comes from the Hebrew words *mayim chaim* (MY-eem KHY-eem), meaning water that comes from rain or a natural spring — originating from God, the source of life (Strong's, "mayim," "chay"). It's not water that's dug out, pulled up, and carried by hand. It's not meant to be stored up for later in case you run out. Little did this woman know that living water isn't an element in the physical world. It's known as *grace* in the spirit realm: eternal life! The living water Jesus is referring to doesn't come from any well, not even Jacob's well. It comes from God alone. You can't work for it, you can only receive it. And once you taste it? You're going to want *everybody* — even "that person" whom you struggle to forgive — to have a great big drink of straight-up, undiluted grace!

When the Samaritan woman asks for some of Jesus's living water, He invites her to go deeper. "Go, call your husband and come here," He says. He's not pulling rank with some move of rabbinical propriety or masculine dominance here. Jesus knows this woman and her situation full well. You see, she's had five husbands, and the guy she's sleeping with now *isn't* one of them. He isn't trying to be proper; He's calling forth the truth.

The woman admits she's not married, and Jesus very gently, very graciously, tells her He knows she's living in sin. This loving challenge has *nothing* to do with her five previous husbands. (We have no way of knowing how this poor woman ended up enduring such great loss, but we do know choices for widows in a war- and famine-ridden Samaritan culture were extremely limited, if any.) Instead, Jesus is addressing the fact that she is sharing her bed with a man who they both know is *not* her husband. Jesus wants her to know that even in desperate times, sin like this is not what God wants for her life.

Does she confess? Nope! She does what any of us might do in this uncomfortable conversation. She changes the subject to anything else she can think of: race, religion, geography, you name it. She knows Jesus has her pegged, but she isn't ready to deal with it quite yet. Besides, this conversation, already wildly inappropriate in both their cultures, just got a little too personal. After a few back-and-forth exchanges, she lays down a response she hopes will pull this encounter to a close. "I don't know about that. I do know that the Messiah is coming. When he arrives, we'll get the whole story" (John 4:25 MSG).

Jesus, not skipping a beat, replies. "I am he, . . . You don't have to wait any longer or look any further" (v. 26 MSG).

Stunned and eager to avoid criticism from the approaching disciples, she rushes back to her village of Sychar, telling everyone she can find how she just met a guy who knew everything about her, everything she had *ever* done. And she asks her first honest, hope-filled question of the afternoon. "Could this man be the Messiah?" The best part? Because of her excitement, the villagers run down to the well to see Jesus for themselves! Before she even *repents*, the Samaritan woman becomes a

GRACE RELEASED

powerful, Spirit-led, grace-filled evangelist. When was the last time *you* asked for a drink?

Choose grace. You *already* have it. It's yours. Release it now. Don't wait until you're ready, don't wait until they repent. Release grace anyway. The kind of radical, reckless grace you've been called to extend is something you were never meant to hold onto.

GRACE REFLECTIONS

1. Why is God's grace offensive in our culture?
2. The world sees God's grace as reckless. They may see you as reckless as you release this gift of grace to others. How does that make you feel?
3. Are you willing to release grace even when the offender is not yet repentant, as Jesus did? Why or why not?

4 Grace of God

> *By grace you have been saved through faith; and that not of yourselves, it is the gift of God; not as a result of works, so that no one may boast.*
> *— Ephesians 2:8–9*

GRACE OF GOD

AN IDENTITY CRISIS

I'm just a sinner saved by grace. If you've been a Christian any length of time, you've probably heard these words before. Made commonplace Christian vernacular by legendary gospel matriarch songwriter, Gloria Gaither, she penned the words to the song "Sinner Saved by Grace" that went something like: I'm just a sinner saved by grace, but He took my place when I was supposed to die for my sins. Now I get to be free and live a great life as a loved and forgiven sinner saved by grace.

It's a lovely sentiment . . . with a big problem. In a word, *just*. That one little word embodies a lie from the pit of hell I'm committed to rebuking. Yes, we've all sinned and fallen short of the glory of God. We deserve death for our sin, which makes us all the more grateful for the reckless grace of God. So yes, of course, you *are* a sinner, saved by grace. But friend, I invite you to consider for a moment, in light of the grace you've received: Is that *all* that you think you are? *Just* a sinner, saved by grace? If that's *all* you think you are, you'll spend your entire life living like you believe it's true, which is called "sinning by faith." Faith is an exercise in belief, and when you believe your identity rests in anything or anyone other than Christ, you'll return to that old identity as a reference point for how to do life. You'll hold on to your old man identity as an excuse to resist the grace of God. And through that filter, you'll never fully receive the gift of grace He has for you. Because if you're *just* a sinner saved by grace, it keeps your full identity in Christ from being realized. It completely misrepresents God's character and His affections toward you. He loves you far too much to leave you where you are in your sin. As deep calls to deep, so He calls you out as a new creation.

GRACE OF GOD

If you don't know who you *really* are in Christ, you'll keep on doing what people who are *just* sinners saved by grace do. You'll keep on sinning, accepting it as an inevitability. That sin will keep you captive as you continually try to repent and earn back the grace you've already been given. Or worse, it will make you apathetic and even *agreeable to* the sin that enslaves you. The enemy will continue to pose the same relentlessly uncreative question he's been asking since the beginning of time. "Did God really say . . . ?" (Genesis 3:1 NIV)

> Did God really say you're forgiven? (Romans 8:31-34)
>
> Did God really say you're adopted? (John 1:12)
>
> Did God really say you're secure? (Romans 8:35-39)
>
> Did God really say you're a channel of His life? (John 15:1, 5)

And he might warp a half-truth from a well-meaning saint as a mortal blow. . . .

> Last I heard, all you are is just a sinner, saved by grace.

I declare over your life: this madness stops today. It's time to let your old man sinner *die* and let your new identity in Christ be your *first* and *only* identity. If you are in Christ, you are a new creation — a child of God, a beloved son or daughter of the King. We were once dead in our sin, but that is *no longer* the case! There is "no condemnation for those who are in Christ Jesus" (Romans 8:1).

GRACE OF GOD

> *You're so much more than just a sinner, saved by grace. It's time you embrace who you really are by receiving God's grace in full.*

AN IDENTITY SHIFT

It's by the grace of God that you are not only saved but given a new identity. And that new identity does not come with permission to remain in your sin. The grace of God liberates you from the power of sin and death, so you can live free in the abundant life God calls you to today. He doesn't want to wait until you feel like you have your act together. He wants to move in and through you *now*. It's out of your new identity in Christ Jesus that you have the capacity to run from sin and choose obedience. It's an identity that leaves sin and death back on the cross where it belongs so you can walk in the light of freedom.

You are not *just a sinner* saved by grace. You are a *saint* — indwelled by the very Spirit of God! "To the saints who are at Ephesus . . ." (Ephesians 1:1) The word "saint" comes from the Greek word *hagios* (ἅγιος), meaning "consecrated to God." Throughout Scripture, the word is almost always *plural*, referring to the saints. You may not be feeling particularly pious at the moment, but God has set you apart for Himself and His kingdom purposes. The saints are quite simply the body of Christ, His church. He makes us saints through His grace and then calls us to live like saints out of the new identity He gives us. Throw out any assumptions about those who have earned a position of sainthood. From the apostle Paul to Martin Luther to Mother Theresa, *not one* of them achieved sainthood but by the grace of God through Christ Jesus. It was given to them freely as a gift, not as a reward for righteousness. And the same goes for you.

GRACE OF GOD

Can you begin to grasp what this truth means for your identity? It means you can *cut it out* with the sinner identity lie! God has pulled you from the muck and mire and set you apart in a place of high honor. Not because of anything you've done to earn a saintly title, but because of God's reckless grace to you and to anyone who believes in the name of Jesus. The grace and authority you've been given come with *fantastic* kingdom responsibilities, including the forgiveness of sins through the release of God's reckless grace. It's from that place of receiving that you're able to turn around and give it to others as Jesus intended. "If you forgive the sins of any, their sins have been forgiven them; if you retain the sins of any, they have been retained" (John 20:23). But remember, releasing God's grace only works in the overflow of grace received. And in all of Scripture, perhaps no one knows this grace better than a woman about to be stoned to death for her sin (John 8).

CAUGHT IN THE ACT

Jesus is in Jerusalem teaching in the temple. The crowds are blown away, and the Pharisees are *furious*. They decide to pull a fast one on Jesus, testing to see if He'll really honor the Law of Moses publicly in light of the grace He is preaching about. One way or another, the religious leaders know of a woman who *at that very moment* is committing adultery. They catch her in the act, drag her out into the streets, and throw her at Jesus's feet. (Evangelism has changed quite a bit in recent years, hasn't it?)

Envisioning this shocking scenario brings up a host of questions. How did they know where she was? How could they possibly know what she was doing? Is she clothed or did they drag her out in all her naked shame? And the *most*

Grace of God

obvious question, *where is the guy* she was with? Why didn't they drag him out too? While we don't have clear-cut answers for much of this, we see they're willing to destroy this woman's reputation and end her life in order to entrap Jesus. This is how religion controls — by finding scapegoats and heaping guilt, shame, and punishment upon them. Have you felt like a scapegoat? You're not alone.

When they bring this broken woman to Jesus, He bends down to the earth in another symbolic (yet *very* literal) gesture. He writes in the dirt with His finger, just as God did when He wrote the Law of Moses. Scripture doesn't tell us exactly what Jesus wrote, but after He writes, Jesus delivers His famous line. "He who is without sin among you, let him be the first to throw a stone at her" (John 8:7).

Reckless! The Law clearly says she is to be stoned. And yet one by one, her accusers walk away, leaving this woman and Jesus alone in the middle of the street. Scripture says Jesus then "straightened up," leading us to believe He had stayed down in the dirt with her the whole time, likely shielding her nakedness from the eyes of her accusers. He straightens up, and then He asks her a fascinating question, one that gives us an even greater revelation of John 20:23. "Woman, where are they? Did no one condemn you?" (John 8:10). It's an odd question, as they both just watched the accusers walk away, one by one. But Jesus isn't asking because He wants to know where her accusers are. Jesus is asking if she sees anyone He can *come into agreement with* on how she should be judged.

"She said, 'No one, Lord'" (John 8:11).

And when she says no, Jesus defaults to His original position. *Grace.* Reckless grace. No strings attached, no questions asked. And Jesus says, "I do not condemn you, either. Go. From now on sin no more" (John 8:11).

The *order* in this grace exchange is critically important. I don't want you to miss this, because it's what we're called to emulate as we release reckless grace as Jesus intended (in John 20:23).

1. I don't condemn you, either.
Before she can dust the dirt from her face, before she can utter a word of repentance or thanks, Jesus *initiates* with grace. He makes the first move. He forgives her. And when He speaks these words over her, He sets her free from her sin.

2. Go. From now on sin no more.
The woman absolutely doesn't get off the hook, but she is invited to walk in the freedom of the grace Jesus just extended to her. In this moment, Jesus puts something important on display.

He intends for us to find freedom **first,** *and* **then** *sin no more.*

When this adulterous woman meets Jesus, she discovers she's not who she thought she was. Through Jesus's grace and forgiveness released, she is restored in an instant to her original identity and lovingly challenged to act accordingly, *empowered by grace to walk in freedom*. She goes from sinner to saint in a moment by the power of grace *released* and *received*. The power of what happens here cannot be missed. You see, when Jesus says, "Go. From now on sin no more," I don't believe He is giving her a challenge to live up to. The very words of Jesus carry the power to create life, to turn on the lights of the universe, to shape history, and to awaken the hardest heart. I believe that when Jesus speaks over her, He is saying far more than

Grace of God

we realize. He is pulling the hook of sin from her heart. He is empowering her to walk in her identity as a child of God, a child of a good Father. She is graced with a supernatural love that will forever be the answer to her deepest longing. Her Savior has refused to condemn her, and she will never be separated from His love again. She has tasted and seen that the Lord is good and now she is free! Why do I believe that? Because that's what authentic grace does. While it doesn't leave you free *to* sin, grace sets you free *from* sin. And if the Son sets you free, you are free indeed.

This divine order translates to our responsibilities as stewards of God's grace: we must be the ones to initiate, recklessly, without fear or concern about how it looks to others or how the individual might react. Why? Because *that's* how Jesus did it. And let's be honest, His Good Shepherd track record is downright impressive when it comes to calling us back to where we were always meant to be. That's what the grace of God really looks like. Here's a recap on the grace process and how it works in the overflow:

1. Believe It.
First, God initiates grace by giving it freely, as a gift, through the death and resurrection of Jesus Christ.

2. Receive It.
Next, we receive God's gift of grace in full, which not only includes accepting God's gift of salvation, but also accepting Jesus's release of reckless grace in His call to forgive the sins of others (in John 20:23).

3. Release It.
Then we can release the grace of God from that place

of overflow and forgive the sins of others by extending reckless grace.

3. REPEAT.

We, in turn, go back to the beginning again, receiving *even more grace* as a reward for our faithful stewardship.

Even as a saint, you won't walk this cycle out perfectly. There will be times you end up striving to release grace because you haven't yet fully received it, raw and unfiltered. Or perhaps you received it once, but you've forgotten the power of the gift you've been given. But just receiving and releasing grace imperfectly doesn't *excuse* you from doing it, nor does it *disqualify* you from the joy of beginning to let God's grace work in your life, however incrementally.

It's time to remember and receive it again — who God really is, the gift you really have in Jesus, and who you really are because of God's reckless grace.

> *God is your loving Father* – one who gave everything He had to reconcile you back to Himself.
>
> *Jesus is your Savior, redeemer, and friend* – one who conquered sin and death for you so you could be reconciled with your loving Father.
>
> *And you? You are a saint* – an adopted son or daughter of the King of heaven and a coheir with Christ; rescued, redeemed, reconciled, and *blameless* in the sight of God.

Haven't you grown weary of teachings that focus more on the fall of man than the resurrection power of Christ and your new identity in Him? The next time you're faced with someone trying to bully you back into that old man

GRACE OF GOD

mentality — whether it's another human being, the enemy, or even yourself — declare these words with authority:

> Yes, I'm a sinner saved by grace. But I'm not *just* a sinner saved by grace. I'm rescued, redeemed, and forgiven in Christ. And guess what that makes me? A saint. I know who I am, because I know who my Father is.

You'll find believing in the truth of your sainthood is far greater motivation to live obediently in the overflow of God's grace than for someone to insist on reminding you of your brokenness. The gospel isn't about you learning to manage your brokenness. You can *try harder* to earn what you already have or you can simply *surrender* to the beautiful truth of the gospel! It's the grace, mercy, and love of God that shape your true identity. You're not a saint because of *what you do*. You're a saint because of *who you are*. And you are who you are because of what He has done. Your identity as a child of God is something nobody can take away from you unless you give him or her permission to do so.

A REVELATION OF LOVE

The reckless grace of God demonstrates a love not of this world. God's grace is His unfathomable love embodied in a person — Jesus Christ. God went to great lengths to let the world know how much He loves us, and He invites us to be part of the revelation of His love to the world through His grace released in and through us. Here's the hard part though:

> *You can't love beyond a revelation of how loved you are by God.*

GRACE OF GOD

You can only love because He loved us first. Even unbelievers can love at a base level. Why? We were created in God's image, whether we choose to believe it and receive it or not. God's love is part of our divine DNA, corrupted at the fall and restored in full in the death and resurrection of Jesus Christ, once and for all.

Like grace, love isn't a feeling; it's a person. It's God. Love is the true nature of His spirit. God is both the creator and initiator of love, creating all things as an expression of Himself to make His love known to the world. Without a revelation of how loved you are by God, you can't turn around and authentically love somebody else as God loves. You won't know *what* love is because you don't really understand the essence of *who* love is.

Do you know how loved you really are by God? Would you like to? Ask Him to show you. Ask Him for a fresh revelation of His love for you, revealed through His grace.

> *God gives you His grace freely, but you only get to keep what you're willing to give away.*

Jesus made this clear after He taught the disciples how to pray using the Lord's prayer. "For if you forgive others for their transgressions, your heavenly Father will also forgive you. But if you do not forgive others, then your Father will not forgive your transgressions" (Matthew 6:14-15). You see, however much grace you're willing to release over others is directly connected to how much grace you'll see manifest in your own life. Because of this truth, you simply cannot give yourself permission to hold onto offense and withhold grace from *anyone*, for *any reason*. The stakes are high. It's not just about your soul but theirs. By withholding grace, you could, in fact, be keeping them

GRACE OF GOD

from experiencing the transformative grace of God. Here's the best part. God's grace is contagious! Once you really receive it, you can't help but give it away. And when others receive it from you, they receive it from God, and they will want to give it away too.

Paul articulates our call to unity in the body of Christ so eloquently in his letter to the Ephesians.

> I, the prisoner of the Lord, implore you to walk in a manner worthy of the calling with which you have been called, with all humility and gentleness, with patience, showing tolerance for one another in love, being diligent to preserve the unity of the Spirit in the bond of peace. There is one body and one Spirit, just as also you were called in one hope of your calling; one Lord, one faith, one baptism, one God and Father of all who is over all and through all and in all.
>
> — Ephesians 4:1–6

God's grace revealed, received, and released manifests the unity in spirit Jesus called us to when He gave us the authority to forgive sins (in John 20:23). And through this unity, we find *joy* – the fullness of God's grace manifest in our lives and in the lives of the people we're called to forgive.

Friend, a day is coming when nobody can steal that joy from you (John 16:21-22). Would you like that day to be today? *Ask Him!* He's been dying for us to ask Him for His grace for generations! If you don't believe me, flip way back to the book of Numbers. In those early days, God told Moses to speak to Aaron and his sons, the priests, about asking for the grace we enjoy freely today through what we now call the Aaronic blessing:

> The Lord bless you, and keep you;

GRACE OF GOD

The Lord make His face shine on you,
And be gracious to you;
The Lord lift up His countenance on you,
And give you peace.
— Numbers 6:25, emphasis mine

As a general rule, the old covenant isn't terribly representative of God's grace on display. We struggle to reconcile this vengeful, wrathful God with the loving, grace-giving God of the New Testament. I'd like to suggest that if the priests of the Old Testament had done what they were empowered to do, they might have experienced a manifestation of grace so powerful, it would rival the grace we have as a part of the new covenant. What have we been empowered to do that we're not doing? Perhaps John 20:23 is our new covenant version of Numbers 6:25. I pray we get it right this time.

We do not have because we do not ask. Jesus said it to the disciples, and He wants you to hear it as well. "Until now you have asked for nothing in My name; ask and you will receive, so that your joy may be made full" (John 16:24). Ask Him for His grace. He's ready and willing to lavish it upon you!

GRACE REFLECTIONS

1. How has God's grace impacted your life?
2. How has God's grace impacted the lives of the people you love?
3. Who do you know who desperately needs to experience God's grace?
4. Would you be willing to be the one to extend it to them? What might that look like?
5. Are you ready to experience the fullness of God's grace?

PART II

THE COST OF GRACE

Grace is free, but costly. Make no mistake: grace is freely given to you by the Father. But it wasn't free — it cost Him everything. Releasing grace to your offenders will cost you something too, maybe even all you have. But anything worth doing will cost you something.

Your money
Your pride
Your time
Your health
Your energy
Your relationships

Count the costs of the finished work of the cross. For God, releasing grace to you, to me, and to the rest of humanity cost His only Son. As you receive the gift of grace Jesus released to you (in John 20:23), it's important to ask yourself three critical questions:

PART II THE COST OF GRACE

> — What will it cost me to release grace?
>
> — Is the freedom I receive worth the freedom I release?
>
> — Will I be a person who releases grace, no matter the cost?
>
> Grace is infinitely valuable and, therefore, expensive. But unlike any monetary exchange we can possibly comprehend, the more grace you give away, the more you get in return. It's all part of the mystery of grace being unveiled to you and through you in Jesus's name.

5 The Problem with Grace

Harboring unforgiveness is like drinking poison and hoping your enemy will die.
— Joyce Meyer

The Problem with Grace

The Disease of Unforgiveness

Unforgiveness is a human disease, one that not only keeps us broken and bound but that keeps us from manifesting God's gift of grace in our lives. When we build up walls of unforgiveness, intentionally or by accident, we sentence ourselves to *soul sickness*. And that same soul sickness keeps us vulnerable to perpetual sin, keeps us from the unity we're called to in the body of Christ, and keeps us from experiencing the fullness of God's reckless grace in our lives.

The only cure for the disease of unforgiveness is grace received. God already wrote you a prescription for this ailment before you were even born, in a quiet upper room with a handful of believers who needed it too. If you haven't already, it's time for you to fill that prescription and receive God's gift of grace so you can have the strength you need to dig into this next chapter. Once you receive His grace, you will be invited to release that same grace in your own life and relationships. Friend, you are not going to want to miss out on this! So how do you battle unforgiveness in an offense-filled world? By releasing grace. Not in your own strength, but as an overflow of the grace Jesus released over you (in John 20:23). Remember, grace isn't a *feeling*; it's a *person* – Jesus. He wants to work in and through you to release His grace and forgiveness to the world.

The problem with releasing reckless grace is that it requires a willingness to position your heart for forgiveness, no matter the circumstance.

It goes against everything your flesh demands in a cry for justice. It's not for the faint of heart, but it is for the children of God. Reckless grace is the kind of grace *only* God can give and *only* God can empower you to extend. You can't even strive to release it — trying harder gets you nowhere. Instead, reckless grace requires your full and ongoing surrender. It means taking a big step back and seeing your role in the larger grace picture. Grace is something you must let go of and let God do in and through you.

REPENTANCE VS. TRANSFORMATION

In chapter 4, we identified one of the biggest lies about forgiveness — that repentance is a prerequisite for grace, and we have the right to hold on to offense until we witness remorse, receive restitution, or see justice served in the matter. The reason offense is still so prevalent in our lives, in the church, and in the world is because we have been given over to the fruit of the fall, which is judgment. As grace-filled believers, we must realign our perspectives with the actions, words, and person of Jesus Christ. And when we do, we find His take on repentance rather shocking. Now before you freak out, hear me on this. Repentance *is* important, but it may not be what you think. For the offender's sake, repentance needs to be more than apologies and penance, more than remorse and empty promises. Authentic repentance is a response to an authentic Holy Spirit encounter that renews the mind and transforms the heart.

> *You can't change your heart, and God won't change your mind. But if you will change your mind, God will change your heart.*

The Problem with Grace

The word repentance originates from the Greek word *metanoia* (μετάνοια), representing a transformative change of heart. A powerfully active word, *metanoia* simply means "to change your mind" — to turn *from* your sin and turn *toward* God. Sounds fantastic, right? Unfortunately, we once again find ourselves a little lost in translation. The history of repentance in the church is *dark*. When the King James Version of the Bible was penned in 1611, the word *metanoia* and its similar verb, *metanoeo* (μετανοέω), were translated as "repent" — an old-English word strongly tied to the Latin word *poenitentiae* — "penance." Shifting the common biblical vernacular for *metanoia* away from changing your mind to doing penance — and adding the "re-" prefix for a *lethal dose* of sin self-consciousness — resulted in a misrepresentation used to justify indulgences; helping to formulate the lie that you could not only *earn* your way into God's grace . . . you could also *buy* it.

Living in perpetual sin self-consciousness ties God's people back into guilt and shame, forcing them to give, serve, and beg for grace and mercy they already have. This backward-looking mentality is not what God intends for you. His *metanoia* has nothing to do with penance and everything to do with grace. This is why God *initiates* with grace. He wants it to be a gift; and for something to qualify as a true gift, you can't earn, buy, or beg for it. Scripture tells us time and again that repentance isn't a prerequisite for grace. Let's look at three of the worst biblical examples of repentance together to better wrap our minds around the radical nature of God's grace.

Think back to *the woman caught in the act of adultery* (John 8). When she is dragged out in all her shame, she says *nothing* in her own defense. No excuses, no apologies, no pleading for mercy, no repentance whatsoever. Granted, she was likely expecting her own imminent death. Most of us would likely be speechless in that moment. She knew she was defenseless against such onslaught.

And yet Christ comes to her defense. He lays down His reputation to protect, advocate for, and forgive her. The Law demands her death, but Jesus has already determined not to condemn her. And this woman has the opportunity to *respond* to the grace she's being given by going and sinning no more. Our greatest revelations of Christ and His character often come in these moments of defenselessness, don't they?

∞

And *let's not forget the parable of the prodigal son* (Luke 15). Talk about your *terrible* repentance! This guy's entire story is entirely selfish: from arrogance, entitlement, and squandering of his family inheritance to pigsties, false humility, and willing bondage.

And yet the son's father still extends inexplicable grace. He sees his son shuffling home in the distance and doesn't wait for him to come groveling; he runs to meet him! And when he gets there, he doesn't even give the son a stern lecture. Instead, he gives him a strong embrace and kisses him, so thrilled to have him alive and home again where he belongs.

The son has no expectation of forgiveness or restoration whatsoever, so he doesn't even ask for it. But the father initiates grace, erasing the son's transgressions and placing him back into his rightful place of high honor in the family. His actions allow the son to remember who he really is — *a beloved child*, no matter what. (Sounds familiar, doesn't it?)

The Problem with Grace

∞

One of the most astonishing examples of how repentance isn't a prerequisite for grace is housed in one monumental event – *the crucifixion of Jesus Christ.* Roman soldiers are gambling for His clothing. The criminals on either side of Him are reviling Him. The religious leaders are mocking Him, the entire crowd blaspheming Him. They're not only unrepentant; they're *ignorant* of what Christ is doing *for them* in the moment. Yet even in his agony, Jesus's concern is for the forgiveness of those who count themselves His enemies. Grace is, after all, the reason He is on the cross in the first place. "Father, forgive them; for they do not know what they are doing" (Luke 23:34). Jesus's prayer in that moment is ultimately answered in the lives of many people surrounding Him that day. In the days that followed, there was an astonishing collective response to the grace Jesus released from the cross:

A. A *thief* crucified alongside Jesus professed faith in Christ and asked that He remember him, and Jesus promised him paradise that very day (Luke 23:39-43).

B. A *Roman centurion* at the foot of the cross saw the remarkable way Jesus breathed His last breath and exclaimed, "Truly this man was the Son of God!" (Mark 15:39).

C. *Joseph,* a wealthy member of the Sanhedrin, publicly aligned himself with Jesus at His death and provided a new garden tomb, as for a king of Judah (John 19:39-41).

The power of God's reckless grace on display in the moment of Christ's death likely impacted countless more lives in the days that followed. In fact, about a month later, three thousand people in Jerusalem were saved in one day as the church began (Acts 2:41).

The important thing to take note of, consider with humility, and remember in our deepest moments of offense is Christ's commitment to *initiation*. He releases grace first so that the offenders have an opportunity to be transformed and restored in response to His goodness and mercy. As ambassadors of Jesus Christ and His kingdom, we are called to do the same. Not because they're *sorry* for what they did. Not because we *feel* like forgiving. But because the grace we carry is profoundly sacred and meant to be released as God sees fit.

Do these people deserve grace? No.
But Jesus gives it anyway.

Do you deserve grace? No.
But Jesus gives it anyway.

Do your offenders deserve grace? No.
But Jesus wants you to give it anyway.

But if you're weighing what we all *deserve* in your grace giving, you're probably asking the wrong questions (more on that in chapter 6). Paul insists the penalty for sin is death (Romans 6:23), but Jesus paid the ultimate price so that you could inherit infinitely more than you deserve – not only eternal life, but *sonship!* And, eventually, He wants you to be able to pay that same grace forward.

Your debt is paid and your inheritance awaits you. It's like finding out someone deposited a million dollars in your bank account – it's yours. Why would you continue to live like you're still broke? Will you receive the gift of grace you've been given?

THE PROBLEM WITH GRACE

WHY IS GRACE SO HARD?

We've uncovered evidence of God's reckless grace in Scripture. We're moved when we hear stories of grace beyond measure in the lives of God's people. We understand the need to *receive* God's grace in order to have the capacity to *release* it as Jesus intended (in John 20:23). And yet when the moment comes, we hesitate.

> *If you struggle to forgive like Jesus did, you're not alone. Many believers do.*

We know we should extend grace, and we may even *want* to. Yet we don't allow grace to overflow as a natural part of our existence. The allure of offense is *thick* in our culture. The sad thing is it can be *even thicker* in the church. We want to be offended. It makes us feel significant, like we have a clear purpose, calling, and identity. As we seek to fill the void in our hearts with offense, even our prayer circles and discipling moments can turn from healthy processing to gossip, if we're not vigilant. Instead of initiating grace and, in turn, finding the freedom we so desperately want, we cling to offense and unforgiveness, and we try to justify our unforgiveness with a so-called righteous anger.

Anger, in and of itself, is not a sin. There *is* a Spirit-led righteous anger that allows God to break our hearts for what breaks His. This includes any evil that is a perversion of His goodness and grace thats trying to make wrong what He already made right. But in Ephesians, Paul quotes King David from Psalm 4:4, "Be angry, and yet do not sin; do not let the sun go down on your anger" (Ephesians 4:26). Be angry. But don't sin. *Seriously?* Is this even possible? The problem is, as finite beings, we get confused. Our anger is more often than not a sinful anger, not a righteous anger. "Everyone must be quick to hear, slow to speak and slow to anger; for *the anger of man does not achieve the righteousness of God*. Therefore, putting aside all filthiness and all that remains of wickedness, in humility receive the word implanted, which is able to save your souls" (James 1:19-21, emphasis mine).

We are God's image bearers. Our image is *like* His. But we are *not* Him. Therefore, our anger is *like* His. But it is *not* His. Because we're not God. This is why it's impossible to release the reckless grace of God in our own strength. It's a supernatural activation moved by the Holy Spirit and released in an act of our total surrender. In the big things and the small things; the most grotesque offense against us to the mild, but nagging, annoyance; grace is God's answer to *His* righteous anger. And our surrender to His anger brings us face-to-face with His grace — grace that invites us even deeper into His image and likeness. Because of this, righteous anger is not a valid reason to cling to unforgiveness. You do have a choice in the matter: God is a gentleman, and He will never force you to do anything. What's more, God's grace covers even your inability or unwillingness to receive it or release it. Even now, in this very moment, God's grace covers you in His invitation to extend His grace. He knows how much it hurts, and He hurts too. He knows how deeply you feel the loss, the pain, the abuse, the myriad of wrongs, and He feels it too. And in that shared space of understanding, He wants to *honor* you beyond your wildest imagination. In the way He did Christ on the cross, He wants to equip you to release His grace as an overflow of His goodness, not a requirement for His love.

The Problem with Grace

The offenses against you are, in fact, an invitation for you to find a greater degree of freedom in this life and an even greater inheritance in God's kingdom come. There may come a day when you look back in thankfulness for the trial God refined you through because it drew you closer to Him and brought you into a deeper understanding of His grace.

Would you like to experience an even greater degree of freedom in your life today? You can — by giving away the very thing that in your flesh you don't feel like you want to give. Grace. A radical, reckless grace that sets both *them* and *you* free. A grace that awakens them to who they really are. A grace that invites them to real *metanoia* repentance and a transformed life that overflows with grace. When you choose to accept God's invitation into radical grace, you may feel less than graceful in the release. You won't do it perfectly every time, so don't place unrealistic expectations on yourself. Especially in cases of severe abuse, neglect, and assault, grace is so carefully interwoven with your own healing, you must resist the temptation to try to extend grace out of obligation or willpower.

If you're angry, be angry. Resist the temptation to sin out of that anger. Surround yourself with grace keepers — fellow believers who won't fuel your offense. Instead, they'll come against it in Jesus's name — even in the moments when you feel like you can't — and they will help you seek and discern God's heart on the issue. The best part? When you give God an *inch* with grace in your healing process, He'll take it a mile a minute from there into the grace overflow. All you have to do is say yes and let Him do the work, in and through you.

The Problem with Grace

Grace for the Unforgivable

"Listen to this, priests! Attention, people of Israel! Royal family, all ears! You're in charge of justice around here. But what have you done? Exploited people at Mizpah, ripped them off on Tabor, victimized them at Shittim. I'm going to punish the lot of you" (Hosea 5:1-2 MSG). Scripture contains a handful of stories that, no matter how deep an understanding you may have of them, they still cut you to the core, every time. Perhaps the most bizarre encounter is that of Hosea the prophet. The very first time God speaks through this young preacher, He has a word for him: *Marry a prostitute*. "Go, take to yourself a wife of harlotry and have children of harlotry; for the land commits flagrant harlotry, forsaking the Lord" (Hosea 1:2). Find a hooker wife and have some hooker kids. . . . *I'm sorry, what?*

Oh, but it gets better. Not only is Hosea to marry a prostitute, God tells him she won't even give up her night job; she'll continue to cheat on him, even after they're married with kids.

So Hosea finds Gomer and has some very depressingly named children: a son Jezreel (God will sow), daughter Lo-ruhamah (not having obtained mercy, not pitied), and son Lo-ammi (not my people). Gomer keeps right on prostituting herself, staying unapologetically unfaithful to Hosea, just as God said. In this account of Scripture, Hosea releases grace over and over again. Is it painful? You know it. Not only to him but to us, the readers of his story! But he can't help it. He has a word from God.

According to old covenant law, Hosea can cast Gomer out for violating their marriage covenant and restore honor to his own name by doing so. This is a viable option for

The Problem with Grace

Hosea, one his friends are probably begging him to choose. But God says no. He continues to reinforce His original position of grace, and Hosea has no choice but to stick with Gomer, come what may.

One day, Gomer hits rock bottom. As a result of her ways, she finds herself on the auction block, moments from being sold into slavery. Hosea finds his wife in this predicament — one she brought on herself and rightfully deserved. But even at her worst, he won't let her go. Instead, he gives everything he has to buy her back again. Consider this for a moment. She is *his wife*. He already loves and "owns" her in a legal sense. And for him to be put into a position where he would have to buy her back again is more than most spouses would be willing to endure. This act of total surrender to God on Hosea's part results in one of the most powerful extensions of grace in the Old Testament — nearly eight hundred years before Jesus, the embodiment of grace, was born. Hosea releases reckless grace over Gomer, grace he could never hope to be reciprocated, given her past. And as a result of that extension of grace, Gomer comes home, for good.

The Judgment Applies to You

Flash forward more than 2,800 years with me and consider another account of grace for the unforgivable, in the story of my friends Charlie and Susie. Like Hosea and Gomer, Charlie and Susie's relationship starts off on a horrific note.

"I date-raped Susie, and she got pregnant." Charlie explains that she wasn't giving up on him. "Susie had prayed me into the kingdom and asked God to give her the father of this baby and God did answer her prayers. We eventually got married." I don't know about you, but this is

The Problem with Grace

not the kind of fairy-tale wedding most people dream of. And even in the middle of this mess, God is moving.

They both had deep issues. Charlie says, "Susie and I both were having relationships outside of our marriage for years. But after my encounter with Jesus, I experienced the genuine love of the Father for the first time." But Charlie still had some rough edges. "One night I made a plan and borrowed a friend's car. I walked a few blocks from an expensive house on the beach. At 1:30 in the morning, I was sitting outside under the window of the house where Susie and her date were *together*. I sat with a .44 Magnum and was planning to scare this guy away from my wife, and if necessary, kill him.

Tragedy is imminent. But God intervenes. In his madness, Charlie hears a voice. *Yes, there's sin going on in there. But if you won't forgive your wife, I'm going to hold her sin against you.* "I knew this was the voice of God. I asked the Lord, "How can this be my fault? Your word is very clear, and what she is doing is sin. If this is my fault, can you prove it in Scripture?" The Lord led Charlie to Hosea 5:1:

> Hear this, O priests!
> Give heed, O house of Israel!
> Listen, O house of the king!
> *For the judgment applies to you,*
> For you have been a snare at Mizpah
> And a net spread out on Tabor.
> — Hosea 5:1, emphasis mine

Charlie empties his gun and repents.

They experienced a supernatural reconciliation and restoration that stands to this day as a powerful marriage

The Problem with Grace

testimony to God's grace. Charlie and Susie have gone on to give more than twenty years of pastoral ministry, seeing lives and marriages redeemed and restored. A sordid beginning nearly leads to an honor killing, but for the grace of God. Instead, we discover what God can do in and through us when we give Him permission to use us as grace vessels, however broken we may be.

> She will pursue her lovers, but she will not overtake them;
> And she will seek them, but will not find *them*.
> Then she will say, "I will go back to my first husband,
> For it was better for me then than now!"
>
> — Hosea 2:7

Hosea's wife, Gomer, gives us yet another classic case of terrible repentance. It's both self-centered and desperate. Even if she feels remorse for what she's done, she's clearly in survival mode. But when she's back in Hosea's arms, he declares truth over her — that she'll never go out on him ever again. "You shall stay with me for many days. You shall not play the harlot, nor shall you have a man; so I will also be toward you" (Hosea 3:3). Hosea's declaration isn't a phrase of demand. If he could have demanded she stay with him, he certainly would have done it before now! But Hosea knows that this release of grace is the moment when she will finally get it. She will know how valued and loved she truly is. And she will know the truth of his heart toward her. He has full confidence she'll never go out again. And she never does.

Hosea and Gomer's story lives on today. It continues to change lives and transform broken marriages nearly three thousand years later, as evidenced by Charlie and Susie, and countless other marriages redeemed and restored in Jesus's name. That's what God's grace really looks like.

Hosea wraps with a powerful end-times prophecy about grace we have yet to see fulfilled. It's an end-times verse *rarely* preached on, but oh, how I wish we would. If we did, it could mean a revelation of grace that transcends what we know as revival — it would be a grace *revolution*. Here's what God says through His prophet, Hosea: "I will also have compassion on her who had not obtained compassion, and I will say to those who were not My people, 'You are My people!' And they will say, 'You are my God!'" (Hosea 2:23). God's words here are so important, Paul iterates them when speaking not only to Jews (Israel), but Gentiles (the church) as well.

> As He says also in Hosea, "I will call those who were not My people, 'My people,' And her who was not beloved, 'beloved.'" "And it shall be that in the place where it was said to them, 'you are not My people,' There they shall be called sons of the living God."
>
> — Romans 9:25–26

Are you picking up on the magnitude of these verses? In the last days, God will pour out His grace on people who do not deserve it. He'll say to those still dead in their sin, *Hey! You! Don't you know who you are? You're one of My people!* Not because of anything they've done, not even as a result of their repentance. He claims us as His own and gives everything — His only Son — to buy us back again because of His unfathomable love for us.

The world is beginning to catch a glimpse of this grace outpouring even now. Marriages are being unfathomably restored, like that of my dear friend, a Pastor, who welcomed his former best friend and his ex-wife, now married to each other with children, to worship with him at his church. The result was redemption, and a family restored to something the world can't begin to grasp. This grace truth moves entire bodies of believers, like Elevation Church in Green Bay, Wisconsin, to do incredibly radical things — like go door to door telling people God forgives them, and that by the blood of Jesus they are forgiven, clean, and holy in God's sight. All they have to do is believe and receive it.

If the response of the people of this world whom God chooses to call His people is anything like Gomer's (and Scripture tells us it will be!), we can expect to see entire *nations* repent in the very best *metanoia* kind of way. They'll turn away from sin and run trembling to God, all because of His grace. "Afterward the sons of Israel will return and seek the Lord their God and David their king; and they will come trembling to the Lord and to His goodness in the last days" (Hosea 3:5). Look at that phrase again. "They will come trembling to God." Trembling *to*, as in *toward*. They won't be trembling *from* — in fear, pain, guilt, or punishment. They will tremble away from sin and *toward* God and His goodness. When they realize they're not just ordinary, broken people but His people? They'll run to Him, trembling at His goodness in the last days.

It's God's grace that leads us to this metanoia repentance. As is always the case with grace, God *initiates* without fail. Our *metanoia* repentance, therefore, is a response to His grace. And Scripture tells us we can expect to see such an outpouring, such a deep revelation of God's grace to this world that entire nations will tremble to His presence. Will you be among them?

THE PROBLEM WITH GRACE

BATTLING UNFORGIVENESS

God's limitless grace is a divine model we were created to emulate. As His image bearers, we have power and authority to walk out anything He calls us to, including grace. And yet in instances of betrayal, abuse, neglect, deep misunderstanding, and assault, we wonder how to extend grace without empowering sin or excusing the offender, leaving us in a place of perpetual victimization. So we cling to our hurt, our offense, our anger, and our pain by withholding grace, and the disease of unforgiveness festers. And when we refuse to release grace, our offenders remain offensive and oblivious, or worse. What's more, we create a barrier between us and God that keeps us from the fullness of His grace.

God desperately wants to bring healing and freedom into your life by meeting every core longing you could ever have — significance, safety, purpose, understanding, belonging, and love — with Himself. He won't force you, but He will continually invite you into something better than your bondage. *Releasing grace* is about coming into agreement with God about what He thinks of others. In His infinite wisdom, He is fully capable of hating sin and loving sinners in a way we, as finite beings, may never fully be able to grasp this side of eternity. But in His wisdom, He invites us to turn away from unforgiveness and toward His goodness. In doing this, He will reveal not only the truth about how He sees us, but the truth about how He sees others. And as we begin to see our offenders from His mind's eye, we can decide to come into agreement with God about what He says: they're forgiven, whether they know it, believe it, or choose to receive it or not.

The Problem with Grace

> *It starts with a simple choice. Choose to honor your offender, in any way you can.*

Honoring people is choosing to see the treasure in them by focusing on something good about them. Perhaps your father was emotionally absent or verbally abusive, and yet he instilled a strong work ethic in you that serves you well, to this day. You can honor him in that one place. Perhaps your spouse has been unfaithful, and yet he or she is still a loving parent to your shared children, even in the aftermath of the offense. You can honor your spouse in that. Perhaps your birth mother abandoned you, never to be seen or heard from again. However, she chose not to have an abortion; in doing so, she gave you a life you can choose to live in the fullest. You can honor her in that.

Even in cases where there is nothing you can find to honor, ask God for a revelation of His heart for the offender. Perhaps a sick, hate-filled, desperately confused young man brings a gun to school, mutilating and killing his fellow students, teachers, and staff — maybe even someone you know and love. You won't know this child from Adam, and you certainly won't be able to rely on the media to share anything honorable with you about the child or his parents. But God, in His grace, can provide a lens through which you can see people for who they really are — His people, desperately gone astray. In this revelation, He may soften your heart by revealing the impacts of bullying and drugs on our youth. Perhaps He will break your heart for the parents, who may have tried desperately to help their child, or perhaps had no idea he was living in such torment.

Choosing to honor your offenders does not excuse their behavior, nor does it downplay what they've done, but it

THE PROBLEM WITH GRACE

does soften your heart and break down the offense barriers between you and God. It heals the disease of unforgiveness. It frees you, and it might even free your offenders as they encounter the grace of the living God in you. Even if they never know about the grace you give, you can usher in an atmosphere of supernatural grace that transcends your offense and brings rebel hearts to *metanoia* repentance.

When you ask God to break your heart for what breaks His, He takes you at your word.

Sometimes He breaks through with a supernatural extension of grace that covers you from pain. Other times, He invites you into refining circumstances to draw you closer to Him and make you more like Himself. Either way, He will honor your surrender and heal you through your willingness to position your heart for forgiveness. You don't even have to know how, because you're not the one who ultimately extends the grace anyhow. If you try to forgive in your flesh, you'll get burned. If you allow God to release His grace through you, you'll be healed and forgiven as you heal and forgive. You may struggle at first, and that's perfectly okay. I imagine for Hosea, the process was a struggle beyond words. Some offenses require time and space to process through forgiveness. We call this counting the costs, and we'll talk more about it in the next chapter. In the meantime, as you walk out your own forgiveness journey or come alongside another seeking God's radical grace, take a cue from Christ, the embodiment of God's grace to humanity: *Only say and do what the Father commands.*

If we only say and do what the Father commands, it takes the emotion and strife out of releasing grace. As

The Problem with Grace

disciples of Jesus, we don't have permission from God to choose anything but grace. Choosing to release grace may not elicit the response we hope for, and that's okay. Sometimes grace and forgiveness bring about restoration but not reconciliation (especially in cases of abuse). The forgiveness may be real and authentic, but the pain of continuing the relationship is too great. But God can redeem these circumstances in unexpected ways. Even Paul and Barnabas parted company, and it led to the commissioning of Silas (Acts 15:36-41).

I encourage you not to put limits on what God can do based on what you've personally experienced. Even now, He continues to reveal more of Himself and His true character of grace in your life and relationships. Nothing is ever too far gone for God to bring about radical breakthrough by way of grace. No matter what offense you're facing, no matter what you're struggling to forgive, ask God to reveal more of His grace character *to you* and *through you*. He longs to give you more of His grace, and as He does, you'll begin to understand that your one and only responsibility is to say and do what the Father commands. And what is His commandment? Eternal life. For you. For me. Even for "that person."

> *I didn't have to fight for it*
> *Or try to get right for it*
> *I didn't have to pay for it*
> *Or have to escape for it*
> *And I didn't have to call for it*
> *Or break through walls for it*
> *I didn't run for freedom*
> *Freedom ran into me.*
>
> — Godfrey Birtill, "The Law"

Before You Go Deeper into the Mystery of Grace...

The next chapter will begin to unearth some of those offenses you're struggling to forgive. It's not an easy chapter. Counting the costs of grace is an important act of surrender in your journey of hope and healing toward grace. Counting the costs is necessary and important, but it can bring about intense emotions like grief, sadness, anger, and fear. Asking God for a supernatural grace covering before you begin will help, and choosing to work through this next chapter with a fellow believer, an accountability partner, or even a Christian counselor can provide extra support and encouragement.

I encourage you to pray and prepare your heart before you move forward. Make sure you're in a place where you're ready to ask God to reveal more of His grace to you and through you. Ask Him to open your eyes to offenses you may not even be aware of so that He can continue His refinement process in you. Ask Him to show you examples of grace that could speak life into your own story, into real life, and into Scripture.

And remember, God is faithful. He can and will complete the good work He has already started in you. He is with you now, and He promises He will be with you until the end of the age.

6 Count the Cost of Grace

*Those of you who do not give up everything
you have cannot be my disciples.*
— *Luke 14:33 (NIV)*

Count the Cost of Grace

A Would-Be Usurper

We live in an intense political climate wrought with lies, deceit, manipulation, and cover-ups. New offenses boil to the surface every day, and the media reinforces these offenses with around-the-clock news networks and play-by-play notifications on every device. But let me tell you, friends, the latest political rant that ticked you off on Facebook has *nothing* on this next story of conflict, betrayal, and attempted murder — that of David and King Saul.

David's story starts out on quite the high note when the prophet Samuel tells him he's the future king of Israel (1 Samuel). But in the meantime, David takes a job as armor bearer and harp player for King Saul — not a bad gig for a shepherd from Bethlehem, the youngest of all Jesse's sons. This role on the king's staff puts him in close proximity for breakthrough.

In all of his tiny glory, David kills Goliath the giant, thereby defeating the Philistines. This act should rightly earn him a place of honor for the rest of his life. At first, King Saul seems pleased, and he makes David head of his army. He even lets David marry his daughter, Michal. And David responds to Saul's promotions in kind, continuing to prove how good he really is when he's flowing in God's strength (a little *too good*, perhaps, for Saul's taste). The women sing out as warriors come home from battle,

Saul has slain his thousands,
And David his ten thousands.

— 1 Samuel 18:7

So Saul does what any jealous king would do in the face of a would-be usurper. He tries to kill David. Multiple times. It gets so bad, David has to flee from Saul and hide out in the desert just to stay alive. We think our modern-day political dramas are fierce, but it doesn't get much more real than this!

Yet even with countless supporters on his side, David still won't usurp Saul's position. David stays loyal, even in the face of death, because he knows that Saul was God's anointed king. He was chosen by God for the job, and God would have to be the one to remove him from it (1 Samuel 26:9-11). David has such faith in God's timing, he passes up two easy opportunities to kill Saul in a cave in self-defense. In fairness, David messes with Saul a little bit, cutting a piece of his robe, even stealing his water jug and spear. He does these things because David wants Saul to know that he *could* have killed him and chose not to. *The grace David released over Saul cost years of his life.* He had to hide in the wilderness in fear, foregoing the honor he'd earned as a mighty warrior and delaying his rise to royalty. But David had a word from God, so he chose to honor Saul and wait on God's timing. He counted the cost of Saul's offenses against him and he chose grace, forgiveness, and honor anyway. This is the kind of grace we're called to.

Long story short: Saul dies, David becomes king, not by his own hand, but in God's perfect timing. Even in the face of death, David trusted that God would deliver him from his oppressor and raise him to his rightful place of honor.

God is not keeping score against you or your offenders, and you don't need to either. Instead, He's weaving an intricate tapestry of grace, encounter by encounter, inviting you into a place of what seems like worldly recklessness — eternally covered in the safety and certainty of His plans for you.

COUNT THE COST OF GRACE

GRACE WILL COST YOU

Counting the costs is a calculation of the consequences of something – a careless or foolish action taken against you. In this section, we'll take a hard look at what's happened so you can understand the full magnitude of what you're releasing grace toward. For deep wounds, counting the costs is the only way you can *surgically* remove the shrapnel of offense from your heart with precision, clarity, and intentionality. Rather than slapping on a bandage while the wound still festers, why not *take care* of the wound by cleaning it out? It not only aides your own healing, it can transform the heart of your offender in the process.

Now it's one thing to identify a cost. It's another thing to use a cost you count as a weapon against your offender. You may be tempted to use what you find as a reason to be withholding of the grace God wants to impart through you. This is not why you count the costs. You count the costs to measure the level of offense you've endured. This is how you can determine the amount of grace you'll need to extend. When you're in full surrender through this process, you may, in fact, become a grace linchpin, as David was in his story with Saul. When Saul found out David passed on an opportunity to kill him, he wept.

> He said to David, "You are more righteous than I; for you have dealt well with me, while I have dealt wickedly with you. You have declared today that you have done good to me, that the Lord delivered me into your hand and yet you did not kill me. For if a man finds his enemy, will he let him go away safely? May the Lord therefore reward you with good in return for what you have done to me this day. Now, behold, I know that you will surely

be king, and that the kingdom of Israel will be established in your hand."

— 1 Samuel 24:17–20

There may, indeed, come a moment when your offenders encounter God's grace through you in such a way that it transforms their lives, and your life, for the better. Saul may have caught a glimpse of this grace, as evidenced by his response to David. He was moved by David's compassion and eventually vowed no more attempts on his life: Saul said, "I have sinned. . . . I will not harm you again because my life was precious in your sight this day. Behold, I have played the fool and have committed a serious error" (1 Samuel 26:21). Ultimately, Saul fell on his own sword after a battle with the Amalekites. David was so devastated when he found out, he *literally* killed the messenger. In choosing to honor Saul and wait on God's timing, David developed genuine, if not complicated, love for his enemy, and he grieved his loss even when he had everything to gain.

GRACE: OLD PLAN VS. NEW PLAN

If you feel like the pain of extending grace might be worse than holding on to the offense, you're not alone. And in some ways, you may be right. However, you have a choice to make. You can stick to the old plan or try the new plan.

> The old plan? *Stay offended.* You can choose to withhold grace and suffer from the disease of unforgiveness, and all the mental, physical, emotional, and spiritual pain and bondage that come with it.
>
> The new plan? *Lament.* In a brutally honest petition to God, you can choose to name the offense, count

the costs, grieve the consequences, draw closer to God, and find the strength to release grace to your offender in Jesus's name. In doing so, you'll find healing of your mind, your body, your heart, your soul, and your will.

Which will you choose? The old plan or the new plan? Here are a few questions to help you consider.

- Do you really want to be a disciple of Jesus Christ? Do you really want to be more like Him every day?
- Do you really believe your sins are forgiven? Are you living in the light of God's grace — grace you know you don't deserve?
- Would you be willing to give it all when it comes to grace, knowing it's the only way to really have it all?
- Are you ready to experience the mystery of God's reckless grace in its fullness by giving it away?

If you answered yes to any of these questions, it's time to write a lament — to count the costs of your offense and prepare your heart to release God's grace.

LAMENTATION INSPIRATION

The book of Lamentations isn't an easy read. It lacks the peaceful flow of the Psalms and the dramatic narrative of the Gospels. And yet for many, these unusually graphic pleas provide comfort. Why? Difficult to digest as they are, they prove we humans are not alone in our suffering. The book does not give reasons for pain, nor does it provide a self-help solution to get yourself out of this kind of bondage. Because if you're still asking *why* or trying to strive your way out of offense by trying harder to forgive, you've missed the point of grace. Lamentations is a raw and real account providing proof of permission to count

COUNT THE COST OF GRACE

the costs of your suffering and air your grievances to God. A lament is not only an *appropriate* approach to count the costs of your offense, it's a *canonized* (sanctioned by ecclesiastical authority) approach. It allows you to process your pain with the Father unrestrained – a necessary step toward true healing.

Whether it takes you minutes or months to work through your lament, please don't rush it. If the grace gift Jesus released (in John 20:23) is a new concept for you, give yourself time to ponder it and pray, because if you rush to release grace before you're ready, it's striving. And grace released through trying harder rarely lasts. As you begin to experience the benefits of writing a lament, you may be able to walk through one in minutes instead of months. But however long it takes you, counting the costs is worth your time. It will usher in the freedom you need to heal and draw you closer to Christ, the author and initiator of grace. And the closer you are to grace Himself, the easier it will be to release grace as a reflection of who you are in Him.

Before you air your grievances to God in lament, you need to fully understand the root of the offense you're carrying. You do that by exploring the offense against you and naming it.

EXPLORING AND NAMING THE OFFENSE

Living in the grace overflow of Jesus takes you from a place of condemnation to a place of confirmation. It gives you an opportunity to remember who you are in Christ and remember the grace He wants to continuously impart to you and through you.

If you want to be authentic in the release of radical grace, you need to fully understand what it is you're

COUNT THE COST OF GRACE

forgiving. You need to name the offense, and that takes some exploration on your part. Think back to "that person," the one from chapter 1 you have a hard time bringing yourself to forgive. Got 'em? It's time to unpack your offense so you can fully understand what you're up against in your unforgiveness diagnosis.

As you explore and name the offense, ask yourself these three important, clarifying questions:

1. Did "that person" sin against you?
2. Did "that person" sin against someone else?
3. Did "that person" sin against God?

Let's unpack each of these.

1. DID "THAT PERSON" SIN AGAINST YOU?

Did people wrong you or hurt in some way? Did they betray you, overlook you, abuse you, underestimate you, neglect you, manipulate you, or place unfair expectations upon you? Did their actions, or *lack of* action, directly impact you on a personal level? If so, let me say: I am truly, deeply sorry. Somebody's blindness has caused you pain, and you don't have to ignore it or pretend it didn't happen. No part of grace means downplaying what's been done to you. *It's not okay.* And your willingness to position your heart toward grace in the situation does not *excuse* their behavior.

But our God? He never wastes a hurt, and He will not forget yours either. In fact, Scripture says our pain matters *so much* to God, He collects our tears in a bottle, never overlooking or wasting even one but recording them in His book (Psalm 56:8). God can and will redeem even the darkest of circumstances, if you let Him. Out of your offenders' blindness, they have unknowingly invited you to experience an even greater degree of freedom by giving away the very thing that in your flesh you don't feel like you want to give them. You guessed it. *Grace*.

2. DID "THAT PERSON" SIN AGAINST SOMEONE ELSE?

Maybe the person hurt someone you love or someone you feel connected to, in one way or another. Or perhaps you simply recognize an injustice and choose to stay angry about it and fight, not because you've been asked to (in an appropriate church discipline kind of way), but because you've simply assumed the right to a role in the situation. This one gets unbelievably tricky. That person's actions against someone else may have offended you greatly. And if God is angry about it, you likely are as well. But if the actions of the offender weren't directed at you, your anger may be misdirected. You have no authoritative right to hold an offense against someone who hasn't sinned against you. What's more, your unforgiveness certainly doesn't help the situation; it fuels the fire and harms you greatly in the process. The person who has been directly impacted may need you as a grace-keeper. It's your responsibility to help usher in the grace of God.

In these cases when the sin *isn't* directed at you, you may feel powerless, desperately wishing you could do something. You can. Your restored identity in Christ gives you authority as a minister of reconciliation — one who brings a fresh revelation of God's grace into the situation in Jesus's name. This is not about grace that you extend personally. Remember, this isn't about you; it's about grace you can release *over the situation*. Know your role. Minister to the offended through prayer, declarations, and compassionate care so he or she may discover and receive the fullness of God's grace gift. Invite the offended into the overflow of this gift, that he or she might release it to the

COUNT THE COST OF GRACE

offender. This is a powerful way to release God's reckless grace.

3. DID THIS PERSON SIN AGAINST GOD?

Maybe you're someone who takes church discipline very seriously, and you've made it your personal mission to restore your brothers and sisters who've strayed. Problem is, when they sin against God, you may find you're more inclined toward offense. You'd rather write them off than chase after them with reckless abandon, as Jesus would that one stray sheep. You may even judge, condemn, and spread offense by gossiping, often in the guise of genuine concern and prayer. (If that last sentence offended you, *good*, it was probably meant for you. Sometimes our hardened hearts need a little tenderizing.)

All too often in the church, we try to convince people of their sin. If we beat 'em down enough, we can get them to come to an altar and receive Christ out of fear. And even after that conversion moment, we keep reminding them of their past, reinforcing their sin-consciousness rather than their Christlikeness. This was *never* the mode of Jesus. He was never afraid to speak the truth in love.

> *Jesus was less interested in convincing people they were sinners, and more interested in convincing them to own their righteousness in Him.*

That's the way the gospel is supposed to work! Out of your restored identity in Christ, because of what Jesus did on the cross, you have power and authority in His name. There's no denying it. Jesus gave you authority to do everything He did, *and more!* But guess what? You have not been given authority to punish, judge, or seek revenge in Jesus's name. Why? Because Jesus never did any of those things either! Study the mode of Christ when seeking to restore someone. Break out that campy, old WWJD bracelet if you need to, or better yet, ask God for a fresh revelation of what restoration really looks like in light of His grace.

NAME IT

Now that you have a better understanding of the roots of your offense, it's time to name yours. Answer these questions right here in your book, or take them to your laptop, notes app, or journal, using these questions as a template.

Remember, if naming the offense evokes strong emotions for you, I encourage you to invite a trusted friend or counselor to walk through these questions with you.

WHO OFFENDED YOU?

Write the name of the individual (or individuals) whose actions caused you to become offended.

_____

_____

_____

_____

WHAT DID HE/SHE/THEY DO?

Describe the specific actions this person took (or failed to take) that negatively impacted you.

_____

_____

COUNT THE COST OF GRACE

WHEN DID IT HAPPEN?

This might be a date (March 26, 2015), a time frame (after my son was born), or a season (when I was a child). If the timing of the offense is significant, explain why.

WHERE DID IT HAPPEN?

Did the offense happen in a specific place – a home, a city, a church, or even online? Who else was present, if anyone?

WHY DID HE/SHE DO IT?

Try not to speculate. Stick to the facts. "I don't know" or "It was an accident" are perfectly acceptable answers here.

COUNT THE COST OF GRACE

DESCRIBE THE IMPACT IT HAD ON YOU.

Describe your pain – the direct impact this person's actions had on you and how the actions made you feel. Don't hold back.

_____
_____
_____
_____
_____
_____

OWN YOUR PART IN IT (IF ANY).

Did you play any part in the offense? Is there any sin or lack of grace on your part in the situation? If so, go ahead and write it down here.

IMPORTANT NOTE: If you are the recipient of any kind of emotional, verbal, or physical abuse or neglect, write these words: NO FAULT. You had no part in what was done to you. Do not accept any blame for what your offender has done.

_____
_____
_____
_____
_____
_____
_____
_____
_____
_____

COUNT THE COST OF GRACE

WHAT DID IT COST YOU?

Calculate what the offense has cost you. Your dignity? Your money? Your marriage? Your time? Your energy? Your relationships? Your security?

_____
_____
_____
_____
_____

WHAT WILL RELEASING GRACE COST YOU?

What will you have to give up to release grace to this person for what he or she has done?

_____
_____
_____
_____
_____

Lament It

Now that you've named the offense and counted the costs associated with it, it's time to do the thing nobody wants to do: let it go, and let God have it. It's painfully freeing. A great way to do it is to write a lament.

Now, before you get intimidated, a lament isn't a complex narrative form . . . it's simply a prayer. It carries the same weight with God whether it's in perfect prose or in a quick bulleted list. The point is to open up to God with the offense that's keeping you in bondage so He can you free you from it.

COUNT THE COST OF GRACE

Use the prompts below to help write a lament to God and air your grievance to Him. You can write your lament right in this book, or take it to your laptop, notes app, or journal, using these eight prompts as a guide.

1. CRY OUT TO GOD.

Call to Him by name and ask Him to draw near.

2. SHARE YOUR COMPLAINT.

Tell Him all about your anger, pain, heartache, or sadness. Invite Him into it.

3. AFFIRM YOUR TRUST.

Remember and list times in your past when God really came through for you. Acknowledge you believe His promises are true.

COUNT THE COST OF GRACE

4. ASK HIM FOR HELP.

Petition for what you want and ask for clarity and discernment on what God wants. Explain why you think He should intervene.

5. NAME YOUR OFFENDER.

Bring your offender before God. Let it all out. Don't hold back – no matter how raw it is, He can take it.

6. ASK FOR HIS GRACE.

Acknowledge that you can't extend grace to your offender without Him. Ask God to reveal any sin in your own life so you can receive and release His grace.

7. Praise Him Anyway.

Even in your pain, even in your anger, praise God anyway.

Try using "even though" and "I will" statements. For example, "Even though this betrayal shakes me to my core, I will praise You for Your faithfulness to me."

8. Declare your assurance in His goodness.

Thank God in advance for what He's going to do in this situation as a result of His grace released to you and through you.

7 Pillars of Grace

Truly, truly, I say to you, he who believes in Me, the works that I do, he will do also; and greater works than these he will do; because I go to the Father. —John 14:12

PILLARS OF GRACE

HERO MAKING

My dad was my hero. A deeply spiritual man, Dad helped usher the grace and peace of God into my life. He modeled "on earth as it is in heaven" (Matthew 6:10) in every smile, every interaction, every act of grace — something I'm *still* learning to model for my wife, Traci, and my grown children, Britain and Sara.

Growing up, I wanted to be just like my dad. And there are days now, even after he's gone, where I see the impact of his life tattooed on my heart. Dad instilled in me a desire to want to empower people, to see the treasure in every living person, to honor the heritage in those who had gone before me, and to never allow religion to quench my hunger for more of God. Dad certainly wasn't perfect, but he knew who his Father was. He wanted to be just like *his* Dad too — *our* God, the Father of all humanity.

I don't know if my family sees me as a hero as I did my dad. In some ways, I'm sure they do. But when you have the opportunity to *receive* and *release* grace and peace the way I have, you become much less interested in being a hero and much more interested in being a *hero maker*. And so I choose to see, honor, and empower the good in everyone I encounter. This applies to not only family, friends, and ministry partners but even to "those people" when they inevitably pop up and give me an opportunity to extend grace. It's what my dad would have done and what my heavenly Father does as well. God's grace is meant for all, and I believe it's my role to release that grace recklessly, like my heavenly Father does, for my good and His glory. Out of my identity as His beloved child, I realize that I no longer have permission to live outside the mystery of God's grace imparted. In time, you'll see it too.

THREE PILLARS OF GRACE

Let's walk through three pillars of grace you will need to believe in God's grace, receive God's grace, and release God's grace to your offenders:

1. passion,
2. process, and
3. prayers.

PILLAR 1: PASSION

Throughout Scripture, Jesus demonstrated an unrivaled passion for grace. He released it with wild abandon and rebuked those who didn't. He came against religion for the sake of religion, law for the sake of the law. And in doing so, He invited people into a deeper revelation of the Father's love for them. Christ was so surrendered to the mystery of God's grace, He was *literally* willing to die on a hill for it. Are you?

As a disciple of Jesus, you're called to embrace and embody His passion for grace, through the Holy Spirit living in you as a grace *conduit*. Being a conduit doesn't just mean you channel the flow of water or other liquid (although that description would be apt when it comes to grace). Conduit originates from the Latin word, *conducere*, which means "bring together." Here's how it works. You receive grace from God through the shed blood of Jesus, you channel that grace flow in the spirit realm, and then you release it as a supernatural overflow of His goodness. *Why?* All for the sake of unity – bringing His people together. This gift of power comes with a responsibility to keep God's grace flowing.

Pillars of Grace

Pillar 2: Process

To recap from chapter 2, the grace process is as follows:
1. Believe it.
2. Receive it.
3. Release it.
4. Repeat.

    The more you flow in God's grace, the more you'll see how the process can vary from person to person and situation to situation. It can be instantaneous or incremental, one-time or cyclical, linear or indirect. However you choose to encounter the process, you'll begin to see how critically important each step is in empowering you toward the next one. I don't include this process here to put grace in a box or give you more rules to obey. Even if you walk through each step in perfect order, you won't do grace perfectly. And that's okay. Nobody *ever has*, except for Christ. Give yourself grace in your grace giving.

    Learning to live a life of grace and peace is a process; it's rarely a one-time event. And in the process, in the waiting, you can count on the Good Shepherd to guide you. As you follow His lead, you'll get a greater revelation of His grace in your life. Others will notice too. This precious season of grace imparted will lead you to a place of healing and victory, where you're poised to usher in the gift of grace for others through prayer, declaration, and anointing. By choosing to engage in this process in any way, you may find yourself in a hero-maker position sooner than you think.

Pillar 3: Prayers

    Love *looks* like something.

    Peace *looks* like something.

Pillars of Grace

Grace *looks* like something.

Or better yet . . . they look like *Someone*.

When you get a revelation of God's love, peace, and grace, you begin to taste and see just how good He really is. And ultimately, that revelation will bring your heart and mind into the place of unity that God longs for His church to embrace — every imperfect, broken, rebellious one of us. A revelation of God's love helps you empathize with the pain in the life of someone else, even if others hurt you deeply. While it in no way excuses the offense, you begin to see that even in the pain your offenders inflict, they're unconsciously drawing another person into their own story.

When people inflict pain, you see a victim making victims. They, like all of us, want to be understood. The end result? Hurt people hurt people who hurt people. It's God's grace that gives us the ability to stop this vicious cycle. Our earthly definition of justice becomes a catalyst for one-upsmanship. It doesn't heal or stop the cycle. Somewhere along the line, someone must be willing to say "This ends here." It's not about excuses, it's about healing . . . for all parties involved. It's hard to do this when you're isolated and enraged. If you're in a deep place of pain, you need others surrounding you to speak life and offer compassion and understanding, the ear of a trusted brother or sister in Christ, the counsel of a wise Christian counselor or pastor, and, of course, the presence of your Father in heaven — the author and perfecter of grace, peace, and love.

Prayer is the most powerful gift you can give or receive. On days when the grace you've been given feels out of reach, for you or someone you're ministering to, walk

Pillars of Grace

through these prayers and declarations to petition a *fresh revelation* of grace from God.

Prayers for Grace

As Brit and I prepared this section of the book, we gathered to pray for you. The prayers and declarations that follow are pleas made to the Father in earnest, declared with authority in Jesus's name over you, your life, and your current reality. Whatever you're facing, know that you were on our hearts and in our prayers long before you read this book. And you've been on the heart of your heavenly Father since before the dawn of existence. Receive these words and be at peace.

Our grace process starts with receiving a revelation of love from the Father. Without that revelation of His love, you cannot truly love and release grace as He intends. When you know you need to release grace to your offender, read through this prayer, aloud, if possible.

God, give me a greater revelation of Your love.

Your Word says love covers a multitude of sins, not just in Your eyes, God, but in mine by my new birthright in Christ Jesus. But when sin and my offense are the most prevalent things in my view, I struggle to release Your grace.

Help me. Help me see my offenders as You do.

Soften my heart. Help me receive Your love anew, so I can impart Your love.

Adjust my view. Help me see and experience Your perfect love for them, because I can't do it on my own.

I confess there are times I don't want to release grace; it's so much easier to stay angry. But I'm hungry and thirsty for more of You, and that means I have to know. Show me how Your heart breaks for them. Fill me with compassion to see beyond my offense and release Your grace and forgiveness to find true healing.

Thank You for Your patience as I learn what it means to release Your grace. I surrender striving, I surrender my works mentality. I surrender trying harder. I know I can't earn Your forgiveness; it's given to me freely, before I even ask for it. Forgive my unwillingness to release Your transformative grace before I see the repentance I see fit in others. Teach me to initiate grace like You do.

Lord, help me die even more to myself and my own desires so that I may live freely in You. Help me embrace a lifestyle of grace — not as a place to arrive, but a gift to receive and flow through.

Give me an encounter that takes me deeper into Your grace. Help me see offense as an opportunity to unlearn everything I thought I knew about grace and relearn it in the safety of Your loving arms. Amen.

ARE YOU STRUGGLING WITH OFFENSE?

Lord, hear our prayer.

God, I know You are not the author of offense.

I break offense off every mind and every heart that's reading this work and exploring Your grace. I know that Your grace confronts offense; I can feel grace confront offense in my own heart and my own life, even offense against You.

And so I release a breaker anointing over every offended heart right now, God, that every heart that's broken would be put back together again; that Your grace would begin to heal, to massage that heart of stone into being a heart of flesh once again; that we would let go of that grip on offense; that we would feel the rest in Your embrace.

As You're not offended or disappointed with us, I pray You would release over every offended heart a divine healing — a supernatural ability to let go of offense. May the clouded, confused lens of offense be pulled off like spiritual cataract surgery coming off eyes clouded by offense. May the joy of heaven be released over offense, Lord God, that it would explode that offense apart, leaving no root of bitterness in any heart, in Jesus's name.

Are you struggling with misdirected anger — offense not against you?

Lord, hear our prayer.

Lord God, we come against the anger that stirs us to sin.

While there's nothing sinful about passion or outrage, I come against misdirected anger that has been used to attach a lie or a label to any life.

God, Your word says Your anger and wrath is only aimed at what interferes with Your love.

God, may it be so with us!

May we defend Your love with our very lives. May we die defending Your grace. May we learn what it really means to lay down our lives for the sake of Your love — a love that saves, delivers, and heals. And in that love, may we release grace — pulling every lie, every label off every life, in Jesus's name.

Do you need God's grace for a difficult discussion?

Lord, hear our prayer.

PILLARS OF GRACE

Lord, I release Your grace over every difficult discussion that's about to be had.

Grace confronts us with the need to have brave communication and even supernaturally led, divinely led conversations.

That may be so uncomfortable to hearts, but God, I pray that You release right now a grace over every difficult conversation. I pray the confusing elements of the spirit that confronted people at the tower of Babel and drew them into a place of separation would be reversed, as when the Holy Spirit fell on us (Acts 2) and caused us to come back together and understand one another again. I pray for a spirit of understanding to permeate every difficult discussion between victim and victimizer, abused and abuser.

May the end result to these conversations be freedom for captives and prisoners and healing for all. I proclaim and declare liberty in those discussions, that they wouldn't escalate tensions but they would bring and release peace in the powerful name of Jesus Christ.

ARE YOU STRUGGLING TO FORGIVE YOURSELF?

Lord, hear our prayer.

God, I pray over all people having a difficult time forgiving themselves for what they've done. Give them grace to see through Your eyes that they are forgiven. They are pure, clean and holy, even if they can come up with a thousand reasons why they think they're not.

God, I thank You that You forgave us long before we ever knew enough to forgive ourselves or others. Your grace has been sufficient throughout time and eternity, so we come into agreement with that grace, even over the person in the mirror.

Those of you who are dealing with the difficulty of forgiving yourself, I pray you will hear now what Jesus would say to you. *I forgive you.*

Therefore, forgive yourself. In forgiving others, you actually release grace over yourself. Lord, let it be that the end of that equation is that we have the grace to be released over others so we can enjoy that grace back over our own lives.

God, I pray for divine intervention into every situation where we're having a difficult time forgiving ourselves.

ARE YOU STRUGGLING TO FORGIVE OTHERS?

Lord, hear our prayer.

Lord, I thank You that Your Holy Spirit doesn't leave us weak or powerless; it empowers us to forgive ourselves and to forgive others.

God, this is not something we can do in our own strength.

It's impossible.

So let us put Your grace on display. Let us put Your love on display. Let us be conduits of Your healing peace and the shalom of heaven to bring reconciliation and restoration.

For You, in Christ, were reconciling the whole world back to yourself in the finished work of the cross.

ARE YOU LONGING TO SEE RESTORATION AND RECONCILIATION IN DAMAGED RELATIONSHIPS?

Lord, hear our prayer.

God, I understand in my mind and receive in my heart that You've restored us back to right relationship with You so that we might have a pure, powerful, significant union with You.

So I release reconciliation and restoration into every heart and life that's reading this prayer right now. May they begin to flow right now to minds and hearts, spirits and souls, and even into bodies — all things made new.

Pains and diseases that have been attached to unforgiveness, be gone in Jesus's name. Healing is flowing right now. Any physical ailment, I cancel that out in the grace and the power of Jesus Christ. I thank You that everything we need is in Your blood.

GRACE DECLARATIONS

Declarations may be something new to your prayer life. If so, here's a little context. The word "declare" comes from the Hebrew *achwah* (אַחְוָא) (Strong's, "achwah"), meaning simply "to make known." When we declare something in the spirit realm, we make known the things we already have possession of according to God's Word. These may include things we know in our minds but our hearts struggle to embrace, or things we want desperately to believe but can't make logical sense of: forgiveness, salvation, restoration, healing. Declarations are a powerful way to speak God's truth over yourself or others, especially when releasing or receiving God's grace. Here you'll find declarations that have been spoken over you and your life.

DECLARING GRACE

I declare the grace of heaven over every person reading this today and any person connected to his or her story.

Pillars of Grace

Declaring Forgiveness

I declare the forgiveness of heaven over every person reading this. You are forgiven by God. The grace that belongs to Him now belongs to you: it's your inheritance.

I declare to you that the forgiveness of God has more power to destroy sin than anything else in the universe. Sin can't match it. You can't out-sin the grace of God.

Declaration of Grace Anointing

I declare a grace anointing over every person as we experience Your grace and forgiveness, God. We, in response, turn around and give that grace anointing away.

I declare that impartation be a daily part of life — through a look or even an embrace — so that we release every person from the bondage of sin, affliction, disease, or a tormented mind.

Declaration of Grace Commissioning

I declare a commissioning of grace over the body of Christ, that we would be a people who are known for love and known for the grace of heaven.

I declare that we would put the kingdom on display by demonstrating Your law of love above everything else. I pray for that grace commissioning to come upon every person, that we would be disciples.

I declare that we would be wholly embraced by, and release, Your grace — like a waterfall of grace, a fire hydrant of grace.

May we use everything You've given us to bring healing and wholeness and freedom to captives and prisoners, in Jesus's name.

PILLARS OF GRACE

The Holy Spirit empowers us to be one with God, united with Him to feel and experience and taste His presence. You've been invited to have an encounter with the Good Shepherd and to be led by His voice. It's my prayer that you learn to know His voice and that your relationship with Him would be one of grace.

My best word of advice is this: As you hear God's voice throughout the day, make yourself available and flexible enough to be bent and shaped by God. As you drift to sleep each night, may you go under with the intention of communing with God.

> Thank You, Jesus. You saved us, healed us, and brought us into that reconciled union with the Father. By Your grace, power, and authority alone, we are yours in grace.

SCRIPTURE PROOF POINTS

Jesus gave you the power and the responsibility to forgive sins. (John 20:23)

God's not keeping score and you don't need to either. (2 Corinthians 5:19)

Talking through offenses and praying for one another brings healing. (James 5:16)

God always initiates with grace. (Mark 2; John 8; John 4)

Grace releases results in an overflow of love. (Luke 7:47)

God's kindness leads us to transformative repentance. (Romans 2:4)

Forgive and you'll be forgiven. Don't and you won't. (Matthew 6:14)

Forgive as many times as it takes. (Matthew 18:22)

Pillars of Grace

God shows mercy and grace to everyone. (Romans 11:31-32)

Anger is normal, but it must not fuel offense. (Ephesians 4:26)

Keep your love warm in the fires of grace. (Matthew 24:12)

We are ministers of reconciliation by the power of God's grace. (2 Corinthians 5:18)

All have sinned, all have been justified by grace. (Romans 3:22-25)

Love triumphs over offense, making us stewards of grace. (1 Peter 4:8-11)

You already have every virtue needed to steward God's grace. (2 Peter 1:3-9)

PART III

GRACE AND GLORY

Once you get a taste of grace, you start to see it everywhere. You almost can't get away from it.

- You'll marvel over grace upon grace upon grace extended to you from the Father.

- You'll bear witness to, and help others release, grace, even when it doesn't make sense.

- You'll begin to feel an authentic desire to choose it, whether it's grace for the moment or grace as part of a deeper inner healing journey.

When grace is all around you, something downright physiological begins to happen. You can breathe again. You can sleep again. You can think clearly again. You smile, you laugh, you dance, you sing; you may even carry a healthy new glow, because God's reckless grace brings about a physical manifestation of joy.

Part III Grace and Glory

> And that joy? It's something the world can't resist. When you live your life in the grace overflow, people are going to wonder what's different about you. They don't know what it is, but deep down, they want it. They may even ask you about it.
>
> And when they do, it is an opportunity to invite them into the mystery of grace through a warm embrace that will never, ever let them go. You are uniquely suited to help them taste and see the joy you've found, the radical, relentless, reckless grace of God.

8 GRACE IN ACTION

When Moses was coming down from Mount Sinai (and the two tablets of the testimony were in Moses' hand as he was coming down from the mountain), that Moses did not know that the skin of his face shone because of his speaking with Him. — Exodus 34:29

Grace in Action

The Glory of God Unveiled in Us

Moses has got to be looking rough, the Israelites must've thought before he descended Mt. Sinai (Exodus 34). And who wouldn't be looking rough after what he had been through? Forty days with no food or water and multiple climbs up and down a mountainside would be certain death for your average eighty-something in his own strength. But Scripture tells us God not only sustains Moses during his time on Mount Sinai, He gives him supernatural strength and a healthy glow that can only come from being in the presence of God. *That glow? Stunning.* So stunning, in fact, it's downright *terrifying* to Moses's brother, Aaron, and the other Israelites. It's hard to imagine someone's face shining and radiating with the glory of God, but Moses has been closer to God than *anyone* since Eden. His face is so scary to the people, he starts wearing a veil so they can still be near him, one he only removes when he goes back into God's presence. God's glory is so powerful, so majestic, so good, the people can't even handle it.

Interestingly, Moses's glory glow began to fade over the years. Yet he kept on wearing that veil. Weird, right? Some attribute this dimming to less face time between God and Moses, but others know the truth. The glory glow Moses carried was attached to the *old covenant* — something that, even in the early years of inception, was already beginning to *pass* away in order to *make* a way for something more. Something much, much better was coming: A *new covenant,* forged in the shed blood of Jesus Christ. Skip ahead to Paul's letters and you'll begin to connect the dots between the old and new covenants. In 2 Corinthians 3, we see how Paul laid out the stark contrasts:

GRACE IN ACTION

1. The old covenant was written on tablets of stone; the new covenant is written on the heart (v. 3).
2. The old covenant is the letter of the law; the new covenant is of the Spirit (v. 6).
3. The old covenant brings condemnation; the new covenant brings righteousness (v. 9).
4. The old covenant had a glory that faded; the new covenant has a glory beyond compare, one that will *never* fade away (vv. 10-11).

The old covenant was never made to last. Moses's glory glow was meant to fade, as was the *religiosity* of the Law he brought down from on high. Unlike Moses, who wore a veil to conceal the temporary glory of the old covenant, we ministers of the new covenant are meant to wear God's *unfading* glory differently, *unapologetically unveiled.* It's from that place of unashamed boldness that we are able to put the glory of God on display to the world, through manifest grace.

The glory of God is synonymous with the goodness of God. And Ephesians 3 says you are the glory of God "filled up to all the fullness of God" (v. 19). How's *that* for an identity booster? God is longing to *unveil* you to show the goodness of His glory to the world, and He wants you to show them through the reckless grace He gives you to release to others. *The church* is meant to put the goodness of God on display in such a radical way that it makes nations tremble, and when we as the church choose to walk in the manner to which we've been called, everything changes.

When you and I get an authentic revelation of the goodness and glory of God through His grace manifest in our lives, I believe we will shine again. And at that point,

Grace in Action

we will be able to say with certainty that we are the light of the world. It's time to unveil your grace glow.

Grace for the Moment

By this point, I sincerely hope you're marveling at the mystery of God's reckless grace in and through you. You believe it, you've received it, and you're ready to release it in Jesus's name. And then the inevitability of *life* happens.

> The barista botches your coffee order.
> Some guy cuts you off in traffic.
> Your neighbor gives you a nasty look.
> Your children disobey you (for the fifth time today).
> An addict you've poured life into relapses.
> A religious leader bullies you back into sin identity.
> An unrepentant abuser continues to abuse.
> Someone you trusted with your life betrays you.

And all that divine grace you've been riding flows right out the window. You think to yourself, *Ugh! One test and I fail?! I can't do this!* And you're right. In your own strength, you certainly can't.

Even when you've experienced the fullness of God's grace — believed it, received it, released it, and repeated it — you may still have times of struggle. This is perfectly normal, even for a saint like you. The ego is a fragile thing, and it can be a powerful force against the grace you want to impart to others. It's hard to get through an entire day (or an *hour*, for that matter) where we feel no offense whatsoever. The good news is, the emotions that come along with these offenses are *real* and worthy of acknowledgment. In fact, they can even be *helpful* as you name your offenses and prepare to dismiss them by way of grace.

GRACE IN ACTION

You see, the painful emotions associated with offense are often symptoms of a bigger problem, an *internal* problem. When our identity rests in anything other than the truth of our sonship in Jesus Christ, we will be tempted to see offenses as personal injustices rather than opportunities to extend grace. The enemy uses our human condition to drag us back into the old man identity, the one that has yet to receive God's grace in full and cannot yet release it in full. And when you doubt for even a moment that that old man sinner self is dead, you make yourself vulnerable to attack. You look longingly at those old chains that used to bind you, wondering if it was easier back in bondage where you could stay offended. Friend, don't believe it for a second. You wouldn't be the first grace-filled believer to look back. Even the Israelites, less than three months into their new freedom from Egyptian captivity, had moments where slavery felt easier than their newfound freedom.

> The whole congregation of the sons of Israel grumbled against Moses and Aaron in the wilderness. The sons of Israel said to them, "Would that we had died by the Lord's hand in the land of Egypt, when we sat by the pots of meat, when we ate bread to the full; for you have brought us out into this wilderness to kill this whole assembly with hunger."
> — Exodus 16:2–3

Hear the truth: God had grace manna for His people in the desert, and He has grace manna for you today.

The God of the universe loves you entirely too much to leave you in chains. His ways aren't always easier, but they are better, and far more life giving than the self-righteous,

Grace in Action

self-reliant ways He pulled you from. He will teach you His way of grace if you let Him, and He has grace for you in the meantime. So as you go about your grace-filled day and hit an offense speed bump, however slight or intense try these tips to help you cling to grace in the moment.

Name It

We covered how to name an offense on a deep level in chapter 5, but as you get more comfortable with the process, it can be done in mere moments mentally. You probably don't need to write a full-on lament for the barista who didn't hear you say decaf, but getting to the root of your irritation is the key.

What really happened? The barista gave you fully loaded java when you specifically ordered it unleaded.

Why is it really bothering you? You're dealing with a newly diagnosed heart condition, and caffeine could mean far worse than a bad night's sleep.

News flash: it's not the barista's negligence that's really driving your offense. It's fear. Before you lay into her, telling her she almost killed you and doesn't even care, take a moment to consider:

What else might be true? Maybe the barista is tired from being up all night, cramming for exams that will determine whether she gets into medical school. Maybe she's overwhelmed on her first day, with a line of impatient customers out the door and round the block. Maybe she argued with her fiancé last night and your coffee is, quite frankly, the last thing on her mind.

Whatever the reasons for why it happened, demanding to know them is not a prerequisite for releasing grace. None of these possibilities excuse the offense against you,

GRACE IN ACTION

but lack of a reason *why* doesn't excuse you from extending grace. And even when you choose grace, it's perfectly acceptable to smile and ask for a fresh, caffeine-free cup, please and thank you.

Releasing the grace of God in the moment requires us to consider what else might be true, so that our hearts can be yielded to releasing the grace we've received.

Maybe the guy who cut you off in traffic is late to an interview for a job he desperately needs.

Maybe your neighbor, an unbeliever, wishes he had a life (and a lawn) a little more like yours.

Maybe your children see you choose your phone over actual face time with them, and they'll do anything for your attention.

Maybe the addict desperately needs to encounter the reckless grace of God.

Maybe that religious leader needs to hear he's more than just a sinner saved by grace.

Maybe your abuser is so lost in her sin, she needs to taste and see God's grace through your healthy boundaries.

Maybe your betrayer is crippled with regret, feeling like forgiveness is something he'll never get, so why even try?

Can you extend grace to these people for their offenses against you, even in part? Can you find some small thing to honor in them, even that they, despite all their faults, are beloved by God and therefore deserve your love as well? "Finally, brethren, whatever is true, whatever is honorable, whatever is right, whatever is pure, whatever is lovely, whatever is of good repute, if there is any excellence and if

GRACE IN ACTION

anything worthy of praise, dwell on these things" (Philippians 4:8).

Here's the fun part. When you choose to extend grace in the moment, it snowballs. When you forgive your neighbor, your pastor, your child — even for a miniscule offense — it affirms the grace of God flowing in your veins. It makes you increasingly aware of the glory of God surrounding your grace interactions, and it puts you in a state of grace consciousness. A drop of grace is all it takes to start a grace outpouring that fills to overflowing in your life and in theirs. Forgive one offense, then another, then another, and bear witness to how much more the desires of your heart come into alignment with God's. You will reach a point where you can't choose anything other than to give grace, as an extension of who you are in grace Himself!

No offense is insurmountable, by the grace of God flowing through you. The glory of God's grace and goodness will be so evident on your shining face, others will see it and, eventually, they'll want it for themselves too. *Grace is contagious.*

YOUR GRACE IN ACTION PLAN

I invite you to go back to your lament (or laments, if you were feeling ambitious) from chapter 7. Perhaps it's been days, or maybe mere hours, since you wrote and reflected upon it. Be honest with yourself. Have you had a chance to fully count the costs of grace for the offense you explored? Are you ready to move deeper into the reckless grace you've been given by giving it away? If not, that's okay. There's no need to release grace prematurely. If there's still work God is trying to do in your heart, sit with Him for a little while. Soak in what He is trying to say to you before you decide what to do about it, and when you're ready to release grace, here's a helpful way to walk through it.

THANK GOD FOR HIS GRACE.

Acknowledge specific ways He has forgiven you and released grace into your life and give Him thanks.

Name the offense.

Tell God how you feel about it, and ask Him to show you how He feels about it. Ask Him to reveal anything that could soften your heart.

ASK GOD TO TAKE THE BURDEN OF OFFENSE FROM YOU.

Affirm you know His way is better than yours, and that you want to release grace for the offense. Tell Him you need His help to do grace well, and position your heart for His loving instruction.

SURRENDER IT.

Asking God to take it and actually giving it to Him are two completely different things! Surrender your fear, pride, rage, and pain. Tell Him He can have it all, every part of it. If it helps, try opening your hands as you pray to signify a deliberate and intentional letting go of your offense.

ASK HIM TO FILL YOU UP WITH HIS GRACE.

Surrendering something often leaves empty places you can either fill up with God or something else. Ask Him to fill you to overflowing with a fresh revelation of His grace. Take your time here; bask in the goodness and glory of His grace toward you.

Grace in Action

Ask Him to reveal an opportunity to release that grace.

The revelation may be instantaneous or it could come hours, days, weeks, or even months from now. It may be specifically related to the offense in your lament and in your prayer. It could be seemingly unrelated yet infinitely helpful on your journey. Whatever it is, whenever it comes, make the choice to say yes to releasing grace as the opportunity is revealed.

As with most new things, we learn grace best by doing. Whether that means trial-by-fire grace in the moment or ongoing daily surrender on a complex, multi-faceted healing journey, God is faithful to complete the work He's started in you and through you. *For you, this means the pressure is off. There's supernatural grace to cover you, even in your grace giving.* Releasing the reckless grace of God isn't easy. But just as a parent would extend grace and encouragement to a little girl who falls as she learns to walk, so will your Father in heaven lift you up and release *grace* upon *grace* upon *grace* as you learn what it means to walk in His footsteps. And just as a child's face lights up in the reflective glow of a parent witnessing those first precious steps, so shall you be — unveiled, with a face that literally shines in the goodness and glory of God's manifest grace.

9

OPPORTUNITIES FOR GRACE

Bless the Lord, O my soul, and forget none of His benefits; who pardons all your iniquities, who heals all your diseases; who redeems your life from the pit, who crowns you with lovingkindness and compassion. — Psalm 103:2–4

Opportunities for Grace

Power and Right to Forgive Sins

Think back for a moment to chapter 1 of this book, where we introduced you to "Paralytic Joe" and his uber-tenacious buddies. A grace bomb was dropped back there, one that's critically important to understanding the mystery of grace. You do not want to miss this.

For a change of pace, we're going to jump into Luke's account of this same story for some revelatory perspective.

> Jesus, aware of their reasonings, answered and said to them, "Why are you reasoning in your hearts? Which is easier, to say, 'Your sins have been forgiven you,' or to say, 'Get up and walk'? But, so that you may know that the Son of Man has authority on earth to forgive sins,"—He said to the paralytic—"I say to you, get up, and pick up your stretcher and go home."
>
> — Luke 5:22–24

Jesus most commonly refers to Himself in Scripture as "Son of Man." And as the Son of Man, He insists He can do nothing of Himself – He can only *do* what He sees His Father do and *say* what He hears His Father say. He, like you, does nothing in His own strength.

Let that soak in for a moment.

As Son of Man, Jesus does *nothing* in His own strength. Although *fully* God, He humbles and empties Himself of any supernatural ability to do anything required of Him. He lives just as you and I do – in sheer obedience to the Father and to the leading of the Spirit. He is still *fully* God, not a created being, but He is also *fully* man – demonstrating the most "normal" Christian life in history. Every time Jesus refers to Himself as Son of Man, He's showing us what is possible for every person freed from sin

OPPORTUNITIES FOR GRACE

and surrendered to the power of the Holy Spirit. *You have the same right and power on earth Jesus did.* To heal the sick. Raise the dead. Cleanse the lepers. Drive out demons. And yes, even those much "easier," more tangible miracles — such as to forgive sins through grace released. Have you grasped the sheer magnitude of the gift you carry?

So back to Joe and his buddies. After his friends lower Joe down through the roof and Jesus tells Joe his sins are forgiven — because of the faith of his friends, if you recall — the Pharisees and teachers of the Law have had enough. They begin whispering, "Who is this man who speaks blasphemies? Who can forgive sins, but God alone?" (Luke 5:21).

Jesus responds to their whispers: "Why do you question this in your hearts?" Do you question it in yours? Do you believe Jesus had the power to forgive sins on this earth? Do you believe you do when you do it in His name, as He said (in John 20:23)? Jesus continues, "Which is easier? To say your sins are forgiven or rise, take up your bed and walk?" This is not a rhetorical question He's asking them, or us. He really does want to know, and He wants us to know that both responses are within our reach.

Then He brings it home. "But that you may know that the Son of Man has power on Earth to forgive sin, I say rise, take up your bed and walk." And in doing so, He releases both healing and forgiveness to Joe, a young man who never even asked for it, as a fulfillment of Psalm 103.

> Bless the Lord, O my soul,
> And forget none of His benefits;
> *Who pardons all your iniquities,*
> *Who heals all your diseases;*
> Who redeems your life from the pit,

Opportunities for Grace

> Who crowns you with lovingkindness and compassion;
> Who satisfies your years with good things,
> So that your youth is renewed like the eagle.
> — Psalm 103:1–5, emphasis mine

In case you were wondering, there's an important reason pardoning iniquities and healing diseases exist within the same poetic stanza. As we see with our friend Joe, Christ has the power to *forgive* and *heal* in a single breath. And as a believer who has received the gift of grace released by Christ (John 20:23), you have this *same power* flowing through your veins by your new birthright in Christ Jesus. Now don't be confused. It's *God* who forgives, in and through you. It's *God* who heals, in and through you. And if we take on the mind of the Son of Man, doing what God does, saying what He says, we will witness the fullness of the grace and glory of the living God here and now. But when we choose to not do what He is doing or not say what He is saying, we deny the reality that He is, in fact, living in us and that we are one with the risen Christ.

Everything Christ did, He empowered you and I to do, including giving grace away. He gives grace to you *and* through you to transform individuals, families, groups, communities, and even nations. Grace is, without a doubt, the most powerful leadership trait God imparts.

Grace-Filled Leadership

Whether you're learning to lead yourself in humility and self-control; discipling another in the ways of Christ; or shepherding congregations, communities, cities, and beyond, one thing is certain. *Grace is the mark of a leader in God's kingdom.* Our call to unity is never more important than when we're in leadership, either by choice or by default. Unfortunately, people often ascend leadership ranks not by looking for commonalities, but by pointing out the minute theological differentiators that keep Christian denominations at odds with one another. Our actions as leaders can either unite or divide, and all too often, we see the latter. By all means, stand in the courage of your convictions. Never compromise on the revelation God has given you, but engage in meaningful discussion with other believers who see things differently than you do, in love. Division and denominationalism are human inventions, spawning from — you guessed it — *offense.*

As leaders, you will one day come face-to-face with the truth — all churches are your church. All people are your people. We are all one body, one spirit. And in that spirit of unity, we are called to grace, peace, and love in each and every interaction we face. The ones you love and lead will follow suit. Grace is key in fostering authentic community in the body of Christ. It's part of building a grace culture I believe we are just beginning to tap into. As believers, we are at the cusp of a grace revolution that will rival any revival we've seen to date, and you, my friend, are invited to be a part of it. Not because of anything you've done. *Because of who you are in Christ.* Because of God's radical, relentless, reckless grace to you and to all of mankind.

GRACE LEADERSHIP IN ACTION

Consider for a moment the places that could use a fresh revelation of God's grace. How might grace transform:

- Your family,
- Your marriage,
- Your church,
- Your team,

Opportunities for Grace

- Your parenting,
- Your ministry,
- Your political party,
- Your religion, and
- Your neighborhood, your country, and your world?

Are you ready to unlearn everything you *thought* you knew about grace and relearn it again through the eyes of your Father in heaven, as revealed through the shed blood of Jesus Christ?

Will you let go of the lie of the attractiveness of unforgiveness and cling to the truth of the beauty of God's grace?

Will you believe it, receive it, release it, and repeat it in the hearts and lives of God's people — *all* people?

This is what grace looks like in action. It was the mode of Jesus, an example He gave us to emulate as children of the living God, and it's what has the power to transform hearts and lives in Jesus's name. And in the end, it will be grace that makes all the difference.

Grace Reflections

1. In what area might extending grace have the greatest impact in your life?

2. How will extending grace impact your leadership/hero-making?

3. What words will you use to inspire people around you to consider grace over offense?

10 THE EMBRACE OF GRACE

God was in Christ hugging the world to himself. — *2 Corinthians 5:17 (CPG)*

The Embrace of Grace

As modern believers, we are blessed with an abundance of translations and versions of Scripture to help us glean deeper and more diverse understanding of God's Word. In many of our go-to English translations of Scripture — including the King James Version (KJV), the NIV, and my personal favorite, the NASB — you'll often stumble on verses with words in italics. And sometimes the placement of these italicized words can seem really odd without proper context. You see, while present-day colloquial writers use italics for emphasis, Bible translators use them for a very different reason. For them, italics are used to indicate English words that have been added to the original language in translation for style, flow, or deeper cultural understanding.

There are groups of people who get all bent out of shape, debating whether these italicized words are, indeed, the inspired Word of God. We're not going to go there, friends; we have far more important grace topics to cover in this final chapter. I see these italics as a gift for English-speaking readers, offering both seamless reading and faithful interpretation. What's more, I find it fascinating to take a passage with italicized words, remove them, and see if the verse still makes sense (or perhaps even *more* sense). I call this "the elimination test."

As you may have guessed, our primary verse on grace, John 20:23, is one we can put to the elimination test for a greater revelation of what God intends with the grace gift Jesus imparts to us. Let's take a deeper look in the NASB. "If you forgive the sins of any, *their sins* have been forgiven them; if you retain the *sins* of any, they have been retained" (John 20:23 NASB).

THE EMBRACE OF GRACE

GOT IT?

If you forgive the sins of any, they are forgiven.

Check.

If you retain the sins of any, they are retained.

Check.

Seems pretty straightforward. We covered quite a bit of this back in chapter 1. But with the italicized additions, I believe we may, in fact, be missing a deeper revelation of the Father's love.

The word "sin" appears *three* times in the NASB translation of this verse:

- The first, "sins," isn't italicized, so it existed in the original manuscript. Let's hang on to it.
- The second instance, "their sins," is italicized, but when you remove it, it doesn't change the meaning.
- But the third "sins" *is* italicized, and when you remove the word using the elimination test, the meaning changes.

A quick and easy way to do the elimination test is to compare the version you're studying with the Interlinear Bible, which displays Hebrew, Aramaic, and Greek words with literal, accurate English meaning placed under each word, line by line. I admit, John 20:23 gets a little clunky, hence the translator's italicized additions, but bear with me; there's some fresh revelation here. "If of any you might forgive the sins, they are forgiven them; if any you might retain, they are retained" (John 20:23 INT).

GOT IT?

If of any you might forgive the sins, they are forgiven.

We're talking about sins here.

The Embrace of Grace

If any you might retain, they are retained.

Wait. Retain any . . . what?

The third "sins" in italics matters greatly because without it, we have a huge question. What — or, perhaps, *who* — is being retained? Jesus isn't talking about retaining "sins" at all in this third reference. He's talking about *people*. The verse shows a balanced, parallel phrasing common in the Gospels, but the two halves aren't opposites. The first half preceding the semicolon and the second half thereafter are talking about two completely separate things: forgiving sins and retaining people. Sandra M. Schneiders, I.H.M., professor emerita in the Jesuit School of Theology at the Graduate Theological Union in Berkeley, California, makes it plain: "The community that forgives sins must holds fast those whom it has brought into the community of eternal life" (Schneiders, *Life in Abundance, 168-98*).

Friends, it's not the *sins* we're retaining but the people — *separate* from their sins. Once they are forgiven in the first part of the verse, we can embrace them in their new forgiven identity.

The word "retain" means to hold, seize, or keep possession of. The late Middle-English term is from the French *retenir*, originating from the Latin *retinere* — a blend of *re-*, or "back" and *tenere*, or "hold." The English word is less about *holding* or *keeping*, and all about *holding back* or even being *withholding*. Language can be limiting, and some scholars debate whether the word retain was, in fact, an accurate translation of the original Greek *krateo* (κρετέω), which means, simply, "to hold" (Reid, *Jesus Risen*, 39).

Yes, we have the authority and right to forgive sins in Jesus's name, but once we accept that gift, the focus shifts.

THE EMBRACE OF GRACE

Jesus doesn't want us focused on the holding onto or letting go of *the sin*. He wants us focused on the holding onto or letting go of *the person*. When we don't forgive, we are embracing the sin itself by refusing to let it go. But when we choose forgiveness, we separate the individuals from their sin. We learn what it means to hate the sin and love the sinner, as Jesus did. And when you see your offenders apart from their sin? It changes everything.

The word "forgive" means to *divorce* individuals from their sin — to remove them from it completely and see them only as God sees them. When we do this, the word "retain" takes on a whole new meaning in the embrace of grace. We are not embracing *the sin*, we are embracing *the person!* The very basis of forgiveness is death and closure to any trespasses against us. Releasing God's grace and forgiveness is about reclaiming mankind's redeemed innocence through the shed blood of Jesus Christ.

So back to our grace verse. The first half is enough, and it's the expectation: If we forgive sins, they're forgiven. Gone. Done. Hallelujah. The second half is the real challenge: If we retain them, they're retained. It's not intended to be negative reinforcement of the grace gift, because it's not about *sin*, it's about *people*. It quite simply means if you *embrace* them, they're *held*.

> You have a choice to make. *Will you hold them in contempt? Or will you hold them in* the embrace of grace *as the Spirit leads you?*

In Scripture, sinners are drawn to Jesus because He is willing to embrace people separate from their sin. His holiness isn't repulsive to sinners, like our own perceived holier-than-thou attitudes can often be. These sinners

The Embrace of Grace

don't even understand the fullness of His grace, they just know they have to be near Him. They'll leave everything behind to follow Him before they even know what they're getting into. They simply choose to say yes to Jesus and His grace and figure out the details as they go. Jesus doesn't hold on to sin or hold back His forgiveness. He holds on to people — sometimes literally, sometimes figuratively. Not letting go of people is far more congruent with the gospel than holding onto sins. We are held by Christ because we are wanted. We hold one another as Christ holds onto us.

How many souls have felt cast away and discarded by religion and church? *Our answer to them in light of grace is clear: We're not letting go of you.* This is the embrace of grace. Christ refuses to condemn. He welcomes sinners. And He releases *grace* upon *grace* upon *grace*. To them. To you. And, if you'll let Him, *through* you.

Freedom vs. Permission

I'm not a bully. If the embrace of grace is a step further than you're *willing* or *able* to go right now, guess what? There's grace to cover you. (Shocker, right?) However you choose to interpret John 20:23 in light of this teaching, invite the Holy Spirit to speak to you through it. But here's the fun part. Whether you see the focus of John 20:23 as talking about sins or people, the *outcome* is still the same. Where in the Word does God encourage us to hold someone's sins against him (or her)? *Nowhere!* How many more times does it encourage compassion, love, and forgiveness? *Infinitely more!* God isn't a bully either. You have the *freedom* to hold on to sin and refuse to embrace your offenders, but you certainly don't have *permission* to do so as a believer. Our wounded hearts long for the embrace of grace, even before we believe it's possible. This

The Embrace of Grace

is why Christ led with invitation, not condemnation. He was willing to invite people in and initiate forgiveness, before they even knew to ask for it.

If you're even dipping a toe into the overflow of God's grace, you will begin to realize that we, as believers, have no other option but to say what the Father says and do what the Father does. We're called to put the love of Christ on display, refusing to hold trespasses against others. Even if we have *freedom* to hold onto offense in our humanity, we don't have the *right* to retain sins as disciples of Christ. The true cost of discipleship is ultimately our very *selves*, being willing to put Christ and His ways first, even when we can't comprehend the *why* or the *how* of it. Our obedience is not contingent upon our understanding of the mystery of grace. Following Christ is an act of surrendering to go where He goes, if for no reason other than to simply be with Him.

> My sheep hear My voice, and I know them, and they follow Me; and I give eternal life to them, and they will never perish; and no one will snatch them out of My hand. My Father, who has given them to Me, is greater than all; and no one is able to snatch them out of the Father's hand.
>
> — John 10:27–29

Surrender is the only prerequisite to being "in" Christ. You'll find, in time, that it's nearly impossible to be in company with Jesus and continue to hold onto your offense. Why? Because it's *painful* to remain in His presence when there's such dissonance between your attitudes. If you're struggling to hear His voice with clarity, offense may be the barrier keeping Him at arm's length (or longer).

The Embrace of Grace

Christ will continue to offer the embrace of grace as we learn what it means to follow Him. No one will snatch His followers out of His hand, nor the Father's hand. We are infinitely and inexplicably held. Our grace embrace is meant to emulate the Father's as Jesus's did, forgiving sins and holding on to people. It takes the word "retain" in John 20:23 from a withholding barrier to a powerful, relentless embrace that's covered in grace and straight from the heart of God. As God is in Christ, Christ is in you, ready to bring the embrace of grace in full for all people.

But What about Boundaries?

This brings us to a critical point where we must ask how we can release God's grace without enabling sin or even putting ourselves in jeopardy. The answer lies in the embrace of grace, a force that supernaturally transcends space and time. You may scoff, wondering how you can *possibly* embrace people who have caused you great pain. I'm not talking about the barista who messed up your coffee or that church member who scolded you for wearing jeans to worship last week. I'm talking about the ones who betrayed you, abused you, manipulated you; the ones you would run from in the street or block on your phone; the ones you know aren't safe for you, even if, deep down, you do believe God wants to release grace to them.

Boundaries are healthy and *very* necessary, but as grace doesn't excuse the behavior of your offender, boundaries don't excuse you from releasing grace. As a grace-filled believer, you need to create boundaries in order to guard your heart and life for kingdom purposes. In instances like these, where you're not sure what grace looks like, you need only look to the mode of Jesus.

The Embrace of Grace

> Now when He was in Jerusalem at the Passover, during the feast, many believed in His name, observing His signs which He was doing. But Jesus, on His part, was not entrusting Himself to them, for He knew all men, and because He did not need anyone to testify concerning man, for He Himself knew what was in man.
>
> — John 2:23–25

Christ gave Himself for everyone but did not "entrust" Himself to everyone. Let that sink in for a moment. He was *for* all but not *to* all. Jesus was always on the move during His ministry, so He had little need for proximity boundaries, if any. There's no biblical record of a restraining order against an angry Pharisee, for example. But when He faced stringent opposition and danger, He shook the dust from His sandals and moved on, and He encouraged His disciples to do the same. Christ didn't need to give Himself *to* all men. His boundaries were healthy and necessary to accomplish His purpose. And yet He still went to the cross to die *for* these people – those who wouldn't receive Him or heed His words. This is the epitome of what it looks like to give oneself *for* someone but not *to* someone. Grace does not require you to give yourself to anyone, especially those who have harmed you greatly and may still cause you harm. But grace does require that you be *for* them, even when you can't possibly love them in your own strength.

> You have heard that it was said, "You shall love your neighbor and hate your enemy." But I say to you, love your enemies and pray for those who persecute you, so that you may be sons of your Father who is in heaven; for He causes His sun to rise on the evil and the good, and sends rain on the righteous and the unrighteous.

The Embrace of Grace

— Matthew 5:43–45

Love your enemies. Pray for your persecutors. Yes, Jesus was *entirely* serious in that mountainside teaching, and His Spirit implores you to the same today. There's a reason God prepared a table before you in their presence (Psalm 23), and it's *not* so you can make them envious; it's so your enemy might become your brother, this side of heaven or not.

It takes a move of compassion to feel the love of God for your offenders, especially when your flesh cringes at the very thought of them, but we are called to love them anyway. It's some of the toughest love Jesus lays down. When we ask God to break our hearts for what breaks His, be ready. He might just *do it*. And the revelation of His perfect love, *for* all, will call you to the same conclusion. Christ gave Himself *for* all but not *to* all. However, He did give Himself *to* a precious few! While Jesus kept Himself insulated from Pharisees who knew *about* God but didn't *know* Him, He prioritized His time with people who genuinely knew Him and wanted to be with Him. Yes, Jesus had favorites. And we're meant to as well! He was willing to give Himself *to* His disciples and a handful of close friends and followers, but this shortlist didn't include everyone. In most cases, it didn't even include His family. He didn't waste time and energy trying to win over His opposition; He chose to surround Himself with the people who truly wanted to be with Him. He couldn't have done it without boundaries.

The lesson here?

Don't believe the lie that releasing grace means you have to give yourself to everyone.

The Embrace of Grace

You can't do it, so please don't try! There's no need to engage your betrayer, your abuser, your manipulators and try to win them over, *especially* when you don't feel safe in their presence. But Jesus was clear that you are to pray for them and learn to love them as God does – separate from their sin.

Creating and maintaining healthy boundaries is between you and God, but keep in mind that severing ties doesn't give you license to harbor offense. Even if you never connect with your offenders again, there is still healing that can happen in your own heart, and even theirs, through the embrace of grace. When you see God's heart for them, it will soften your own heart toward them. You'll be able to love them with His perfect love, His perfect grace manifest within you. That kind of love transcends space and time, releasing reckless grace from wherever you are to wherever they are.

Giving ourselves *to* someone calls for an investment in time, energy, responsibility, and love. Giving yourself *for* others means laying down your life for them, even in their brokenness. It's a death to self few believers are comfortable with, but all of us are called to it. Does this mean continuing to endure abuse? *Absolutely not!* But it does mean loving the abusers as persons, apart from their sin. It's a sacrificial love that positions your heart for deeper healing as you let God's grace flow through you. When you find clarity from God on what grace looks like in your situation, you may experience strong opinions, or even opposition, from well-meaning saints around you. They may call you reckless, and if they do, you know you're probably on the right track. When this happens, take a hint from Paul's first letter to the church in Corinth (1 Corinthians 4:3). You don't need to be worried about what

The Embrace of Grace

others think about you, and, quite frankly, you don't even need to be worried about what *you* think of yourself. God's opinion is the only one that matters.

> *The embrace of grace is about coming into agreement with God in Christ, and Christ in you, by being unapologetically for* all, *but not to* all.

When you come into agreement with God in this way, He will move your heart to a place of deeper healing; a place where you truly *want* to see redemption, restoration, and, perhaps, even reconciliation in the life of your offender. When grace seems impossible, keep in mind that God *loves a challenge*. And you never want to underestimate the kind of kingdom breakthrough He *can* and *will* bring through your heart posture alone.

Love-Based Prioritization

Even in your desire to release God's reckless grace, keep in mind that no human relationship is meant to be prioritized above our relationship with the Father. When scribes asked Jesus which commandment was first and foremost, He made it plain.

> Jesus answered, "The foremost is, 'Hear, O Israel! The Lord our God is one Lord; and you shall love the Lord your God with all your heart, and with all your soul, and with all your mind, and with all your strength.' The second is this, 'You shall love your neighbor as yourself.' There is no other commandment greater than these."
> — Mark 12:29–32

Jesus prioritized His time, energy, and affections for the people who wanted to be with Him most. He absolutely had favorites — about seventy regular followers, twelve disciples, and an inner circle of three: Peter, James, and John. This resulted in rivalries among His followers, but in the end provided them with the deep investment they needed to become disciples who knew how to *make* disciples — by being *for* all and *to* a precious few. But above each of these beloved brothers and sisters, Jesus regularly and sometimes quite *unexpectedly* stole Himself away to be with the Father. Here's how Jesus's love-based prioritization model worked.

Priority 1. Love God.

Love Him with *all* your heart, *all* your soul, *all* your mind, *all* your strength. Yes, *all* of yourself. You see, when God is first on your list of priorities, love is no longer a finite resource, it's infinitely renewable. You can give Him everything you have and He refills you with *even more* love and grace than you had in the first place — so much, you can't hold it all in; you *have* to give it away.

Priority 2. Love your people of peace.

These are the precious few you give yourself *to*, the relationships you invest significant time and energy into. It could be your spouse, a dear friend, someone you disciple, or someone who disciples you. You invite and challenge one another appropriately, just as Jesus modeled with His disciples. They *want* to be with you and you *want* to be with them.

The Embrace of Grace

Priority 3. Love Everyone Else.

These people are your "neighbors," the ones Jesus commanded us to love as ourselves. They may be friendly neighbors you wave to while checking the mail, or perhaps they're not very neighborly at all — one may be an offender, or even an abuser. You might not invest significant time and energy into winning them over, and that may be for the best. And although you are not called to give yourself *to* them, you are called to give your life *for* them, as Jesus did.

Jesus's example shows you that you, too, are meant to prioritize who you will give yourself *to* (John 2:24). You're meant to have favorites, but if any person of peace, or even a neighbor, begins to steal margin away from God, it's time to reprioritize. This means saying yes to God and no to anything that distracts you from His calling on your life. Follow Jesus's model and, in time, you'll be less worried about creating fear-based boundaries to keep you insulated from offenders, not-so-neighborly neighbors, and even abusers. You'll find yourself more focused on love-based prioritization and choosing to be fully present during each unique encounter you're given.

Sympathy vs. Compassion

A final word of caution for the embrace of grace: check your heart motives. Are you being driven by sympathy or compassion? The answer you give may dramatically impact the fruit you see.

> *Sympathy* is a feeling of pity or sorrow for others, or perhaps some understanding of what they are going through. We all feel sympathy at times, and it's not a wrong feeling, but it's important to acknowledge that sympathy is powerless — it's all heart, no solutions.

The Embrace of Grace

When we move out of sympathy, we move in our own strength, full of fear, brokenness, and strife.

Compassion, on the other hand, is an empowering force. God moved Jesus with compassion before He performed His greatest miracles. Fully human by choice, Jesus had no option but to wait on God to *move* Him with the compassion of heaven.

When we move out of compassion, we move as one with God, full of power, love, and grace.

You may think I'm splitting hairs here, but know this truth: grace is *not* sympathy; grace is genuine compassion, moved by the hand of God.

We live in a sympathy addicted culture. We can barely make it through breakfast without hearing five heart-wrenching news stories we wish we could do something about. But imposing solutions when we feel sympathetic won't do anything to change the situation. Conversely, it can even lead you to enable poor decisions and bad behavior as you try to fix, save, or comfort beyond your calling. Even worse, it can lead those who are suffering to love and rely on *you* more than they love and rely on God. Sympathy can, in fact, do more harm than good.

As believers, we are allowed to care, and we certainly *should* care. I pray you really *do* care. And yet there will be some stories we sympathize with but others that move us with compassion to release grace over the situation through prayer, support, or some specific action. We cannot possibly give ourselves *to* all people who are hurting, but we can give ourselves *for* all. We are moved with compassion to release grace over specific people or situations.

THE EMBRACE OF GRACE

As you get caught up in the embrace of grace, the enormity of the opportunity can feel overwhelming. Start small. Focus on the person right in front of you. Be open to the leading of the Holy Spirit as you discern who to give yourself *to* and *for*. And stay flexible enough to be moved with compassion when God calls you to rise up and release His grace.

CHOOSE GRACE. IT'S THAT SIMPLE.

You already have the gift of grace. It's been yours since before you were born. The time has come for you, me, and all followers of Christ to believe it, receive it, release it, and repeat. You will never be ready in your flesh, only by God's spirit within you. Release grace as soon as you possibly can. You don't need to wait until you *feel* like you're ready. Feelings are deceptive. Make grace a conscious choice of surrender, not a feelings-based reaction. You won't do grace perfectly, and that's okay. The goal isn't perfection, it's refinement.

Jesus meant what He said about forgiveness (in John 20:23), and as God's beloved sons and daughters, we have been invited to be a part of what He is doing — bringing His kingdom through the impartation and release of grace through the forgiveness of sins. We are held in the embrace of grace and meant to invite others in, as "God [is] in Christ hugging the world to himself" (2 Corinthians 5:17 CPG). God in Christ, Christ in you. You are an ambassador of grace. And when you choose to believe it's true? I believe you will see reckless, inexplicable grace manifest in your own life and situations, and beyond. We will become grace apostles, instrumental in raising up a generation of grace-filled believers poised to bring God's kingdom in its fullness as part of an in-breaking grace

THE EMBRACE OF GRACE

revolution in the church. It's going to be a revival unlike anything you've witnessed before. Religiosity, denominationalism, and "churchianity" will be gone, in Jesus's name, and replaced by an authentic desire for unity in the body of Christ. Trust me, friend, you do not want to miss this!

ARE YOU READY?

By God's reckless grace, yes, you are.

1. Believe it.
2. Receive it.
3. Release it.
4. Repeat.

GRACE REFLECTIONS

Grace works best in a community of believers. Take a moment to create a shortlist of people of peace who you know will surround you and encourage you to release grace.

Who welcomes you?
Who do you feel safe with?
Who invests in you regularly?
Who understands your offense?
Who wants to help you heal?

Write their names here. My people of peace are:

WORKS CITED

CHAPTER 1

Hatch, Edwin. "Breathe on Me, Breath of God." 1878. In *Allon's Congregational Psalmist Hymnal*. Whitsuntide, 1886. Public domain.

McClarney, Chris. "Blow Mighty Breath of God." *Love Never Fails*. Integrity Music, 2009.

"H127 - 'adamah - Strong's Hebrew Lexicon (NASB)." Blue Letter Bible. Accessed 31 Oct, 2018. https://www.blueletterbible.org//lang/lexicon/lexicon.cfm?Strongs=h127&t=NASB.

CHAPTER 3

"G5373 - philia - Strong's Greek Lexicon (NASB)." Blue Letter Bible. Accessed 31 Oct, 2018. https://www.blueletterbible.org//lang/lexicon/lexicon.cfm?Strongs=g5373&t=NASB.

"G5387 - philostorgos - Strong's Greek Lexicon (NASB)." Blue Letter Bible. Accessed 6 Nov, 2018. https://www.blueletterbible.org//lang/lexicon/lexicon.cfm?Strongs=g5387&t=NASB.

"G5318 - phaneros - Strong's Greek Lexicon (NASB)." Blue Letter Bible. Accessed 6 Nov, 2018. https://www.blueletterbible.org//lang/lexicon/lexicon.cfm?Strongs=g5318&t=NASB.

"G26 - agapē - Strong's Greek Lexicon (NASB)." Blue Letter Bible. Accessed 31 Oct, 2018.

https://www.blueletterbible.org//lang/lexicon/lexicon.cfm?Strongs=g26&t=NASB.

"G5368 - phileō - Strong's Greek Lexicon (NASB)." Blue Letter Bible. Accessed 31 Oct, 2018. https://www.blueletterbible.org//lang/lexicon/lexicon.cfm?Strongs=g5368&t=NASB.

"H4325 - mayim - Strong's Hebrew Lexicon (NASB)." Blue Letter Bible. Accessed 31 Oct, 2018. https://www.blueletterbible.org//lang/lexicon/lexicon.cfm?Strongs=h4325&t=NASB.

"H2416 - chay - Strong's Hebrew Lexicon (NASB)." Blue Letter Bible. Accessed 31 Oct, 2018. https://www.blueletterbible.org//lang/lexicon/lexicon.cfm?Strongs=h2416&t=NASB.

CHAPTER 5

"G3341 - metanoia - Strong's Greek Lexicon (NASB)." Blue Letter Bible. Accessed 31 Oct, 2018. https://www.blueletterbible.org//lang/lexicon/lexicon.cfm?Strongs=g3341&t=NASB.

CHAPTER 7

"H262 - 'achvah - Strong's Hebrew Lexicon (NASB)." Blue Letter Bible. Accessed 2 Nov, 2018. https://www.blueletterbible.org//lang/lexicon/lexicon.cfm?Strongs=h262&t=NASB.

CHAPTER 10

Reid, Barbara E. Abiding Word: Sunday Reflections for Year B. Liturgical Press, 2011.

Sandra Marie Schneiders, "The Resurrection (of the Body) in the Fourth Gospel: A Key to Johannine Spirituality," in Life in Abundance: Studies of John's Gospel in Tribute to Raymond E. Brown, ed. John R. Donahue. Collegeville, MN: Liturgical Press, 2005.

About Bill

Bill Vanderbush is a third-generation minister who has pastored for over twenty-five years. He and his wife, Traci, had a supernatural encounter with the Holy Spirit that drew them into an incredible adventure of being shaped and fashioned by the power and grace of God.

Bill's consuming passion is to empower people to do the greater works that Jesus spoke of and live out the mystery of our union with Christ. Bill and Traci's ministry invites people into a spontaneous, Holy Spirit-led, team ministry training experience that will forever transform the way you see and do life. Through this message and revelation of the grace of God, you will be liberated and empowered to invade the impossible.

Bill and Traci currently live in Celebration, Florida. They have two grown children, Britain and Sara.

Contact Bill

FACEBOOK: www.facebook.com/billvanderbushpublic

WEBSITE: www.billvanderbush.com
www.vanderbushministries.com

INSTAGRAM: www.instagram.com/billosopher59

TWITTER: www.twitter.com/BillVanderbush

PODCAST: www.vanderbushministries.com/Vanderbush_Ministries/Podcast/Podcast.html

About Brit

Brit Eaton is a writer, speaker, discipler, and all-around pursuer of the kingdom of God. She helps corporate, nonprofit, and ministry leaders find the words to say to move people to action. An eager apostle and strong advocate for women in ministry, Brit thrives in diverse, Spirit-filled environments committed to unity in the body of Christ.

Brit lives with her husband, Mike, and daughter, Bella, in Mount Vernon, Ohio.

Contact Brit

FACEBOOK: facebook.com/briteaton

WEBSITE: www.briteaton.com

CAN YOU HELP?

Reviews are everything to an author, because they mean a book is given more visibility. If you enjoyed this book, please review it on your favorite book review sites and tell your friends about it. Thank you!

Bill's Teaching Materials

Project 24 is sold at live events as a USB flash drive and contains more than twenty-four hours of teaching that will impact your perspective of your identity in Christ from a wide variety of angles. Upon purchase, you will be sent a link to a web page where you can stream or download all twenty-four hours of the audio and video files.

Messages Include:
- Stewarding the Grace of God
- Out of the Wilderness in the Power of the Spirit
- You Are the Glory That Covers the Earth
- Understanding the Mysteries of God
- Being Love in the Darkness
- Walking in Identity and Authority
- Living Free from a Sin Conscious Mentality
- The Vengeance of God
- What Does God Believe about You?
- Empowering Women in Ministry
- Walking in the Ultimate Inheritance

and many more.

BUY AT: www.billvanderbush.com/resources-1

PRESENCE AND POWER

Presence and Power is sold at live events as a USB flash drive and contains more than twelve hours of teaching on walking in the supernatural life that Jesus Christ has given to you. This download also includes PDF files of notes for some of the messages. Upon purchase, you will be sent a link to a web page, where you can stream or download all twelve hours of the audio and PDF files.

Messages Include:
- Spiritual Joyfare
- Overcoming Demonic Influence
- Living in the Presence
- Being a Student of the Spirit
- Greater Works Will You Do
- Increasing in Favor
- Words of Knowledge
- Healing and Miracles

and many more.

BUY AT: www.billvanderbush.com/resources-1

VIGNETTE: GLIMPSES OF MYSTERIOUS LOVE

by Traci A. Vanderbush (Author),
William H. Vanderbush (Contributor)

Raw, unstructured, free-flowing. Love is an indefinable mystery. This is one couple's attempt, after learning the art of falling in love with each other once again, to articulate the limitless depths of the human soul. Through various journal entries, thoughts, and poetic expressions regarding love, mercy, grace, and sexuality; join them on this journey of glimpses into mysterious love.

BUY AT: www.billvanderbush.com/resources-1

Made in the USA
San Bernardino, CA
14 December 2018